INDIAN SCULPTURE

Bhū Devī
S. India
14th-15th Century
[See Pl. 53]

INDIAN SCULPTURE

IN THE PHILADELPHIA MUSEUM OF ART

STELLA KRAMRISCH

PHILADELPHIA • UNIVERSITY OF PENNSYLVANIA PRESS

Published in Great Britain, India, and Pakistan
by the Oxford University Press
London, Bombay, and Karachi

Library of Congress Catalog Card Number: 60–14837

This publication has been made possible in part by a grant from the CATHERWOOD FOUNDATION and by bequest of HORTENSE F. LOEB.

Photographs: A. J. Wyatt

Printed in the United States of America

Contents

Note on Pronunciation

The letter **c** in Indian words is pronounced as **ch**; **ś** and **ṣ** as **sh**; **ṛ** as **r**.

Diacritical marks on place names are given only where they are necessary to avoid mispronunciation.

Introduction

THE INDIAN SCULPTURES in the Philadelphia Museum of Art date approximately from the first century B.C. to the nineteenth century A.D. The early schools are represented by a few examples only. Most of the sculptures were created in the centuries of the great stone temples (seventh to thirteenth century and in South India to the seventeenth century) in such centres as Bhuvaneshvar in Orissa in the extreme East; Khajurāho in the "midland" of Madhya Pradesh; Kiradu in Rājasthān in the West; and Madura in the far South. Widely distributed through space and time, the sculptures are the work of various schools, produced at different phases of their maturity. At the same time and irrespective of their distinctions, they are unmistakably Indian by virtue of their particular kind of plasticity.

The sculptures in the Museum are detached from their original context. They were each part of a larger monument, a special kind of sanctuary or a temple. These monuments had their definite function and meaning. Within its own integrity, each sculpture was part of their total form. The monument with its sculpture was complete in its concreteness when it was seen and used. It was seen with the eye of knowledge and used with ritual competence.

The single sculpture as a work of art in itself and as part of a larger context is the final stage of the inspiration, method, and skill of the Indian artist. As substantiated inspiration the form of each sculpture confronts the onlooker with the power that went into its making. The form is essentially plastic. Viewing and accounting to himself for the particular plasticity of Indian sculpture, the onlooker by way of re-creation may reinvest the sculptures with the concreteness of their intended effect.

INDIAN SCULPTURE

1

Plastic Symbols

ACCORDING TO INDIAN knowledge, everything exists on three levels of reference: the gross or physical; the subtle, where the emotions and senses hold sway; and the level of the spirit above and beyond the other two. Because in Indian sculpture the accent is not on physical reality, the subtle world of the senses and emotions enthralls the spirit. It endows the spirit with a body, made by art in a concrete material. This body is the plastic form in which the sculptured images and symbols exist. The images, which are those of divinity and which were worshipped, are called "mūrti." Mūrti means "concrete." A mūrti is the concrete shape of an invisible inner realisation, of a transcendent vision. It is the body in which a god is made real.

Buddhist Mahāyāna doctrine speaks of the Nirmāṇa-kāya, a body of manifestation, the extended, measurable (nir-māṇa) body which the Buddha, the transcendental principle, assumes in order to be manifest to man. This apparitional and phenomenal body, from the point of ultimate reality, is an "assumption," a taking upon itself by the ultimate and invisibly Real the lineaments of the illusory world of appearance.

In the Nirmāṇa-kāya the transcendent principle becomes real to the understanding of those who see that body. The Buddha image is such a Nirmāṇa-kāya, a "measured out body" assumed by the Buddha and given to him by the concrete work of the artist. In order to make this gift and presentation, the artist draws on what he knows and has seen, for in this way only can he make others see and understand.

He makes them see and understand an invisible content. The invisible content of the work-of-art-to-be is realised inwardly by the artist. Within him takes place the progression of the content of the work of art from its invisible state into the concrete form of the work of art. This progression has three levels. On the first and highest level an invisibly Real seizes the creativeness of the sculptor. In the embrace of the creativeness of the sculptor, the invisibly Real now pervades the "subtle body" of his inner experience, and becomes plastic form. On this level the plastic form, in its flux and tendency to become concrete, draws to itself what the artist sees of the outer world. The plastic form remolds and transforms the data of the outer world and incorporates them in the concrete image (mūrti). On this last level the data of the outer world, having been lifted by the artist from their objects, are absorbed in the plastic form or creative substance. It is there that they enter into manifold configurations.

Among the recurrent configurations of Indian sculpture, three belong to all the ages of Indian art over the last two thousand years. They are the combined man-animal shape (Pl. 54), the woman and tree configuration (Pl. 38), and the group of man and woman in union (Pl. 17). The man-animal shape is not exclusively Indian. It is known to palaeolithic cave painting, to Mesopotamian, Egyptian and Greek art, to the Renaissance. Even today, the Minotaur lives in the art of Picasso. In India the man-animal shapes of the gods are worshipped to this day in their ancient configurations which the sculptors of all ages endowed with ever new plastic form.

Each of the three perennially recurrent configurations presents, as one visual conception, two conjoint principles separate in their natures. Conjoined, they interpenetrate, the one being raised to the power of the other. The effect of their increased powers is strengthened by their contrast, as well as by their fusion, in one form. Such wholeness of power-charged contrasts stands for divine power, as it is felt in man and in the cosmos. An image of elephant-headed Gaṇeśa (Pl. 54), the "Lord of Hosts," is, according to Indian tradition, an embodiment of transcendental power and immanent power whose particular quality is conveyed by the specific animal shape in configuration with that of man.

The man-animal configuration joins part to part, one of the animal, the other of man, into the presence of a god. Each of the other two types of conjoint shape preserves the integrity of its parts, whether in the configuration of woman and tree, which is known by the name of the theme as that of the tree-woman (Śālabhañjikā), or of man and woman in union (Mithuna). But whether built up of parts combined by art into a new creature or composed of two separate figures in nearness or embrace, the configuration has visual wholeness. The man-animal configuration has a plausible form, for the figure of man in Indian sculpture, being a vessel of the life breath, is akin, in this respect, to that of the animal and can be inflated or compressed to animal proportions. The male body in Indian art is given its perfection when it has the waist of a lion and the shoulders of an elephant.

The awareness of this affinity inherent in the shapes of nature is transposed in sculpture. Becoming resorbed on the subtle level into the inner plastic form of the life breath, the resorbed awareness partakes of the invisibly Real that pervades the plastic form and compels the artist to create the concrete work. When completed the concrete work has its effect on the physical, the subtle, and transcendental planes. The work of art, the concrete image, exists on these three levels.

The image of Gaṇeśa, the popular and mysterious god, has an elephant head and a man's portly body (Pl. 54). Gaṇeśa does not exist without his image; he is seen as image and is made an image. Seeing and thinking in images are one. As a "concrete thought image"—this contradiction being no more paradoxical than the shape of the god—the effect of the sculpture is valid on the three planes of reference, and the existence of Gaṇeśa is their link. The coagulated plastic volume of elephant head and body of man symbolizes the coherence of the universe, the macrocosm, and of man, the microcosm. The elephant head in its largeness refers to the macrocosm and the body of man to the microcosm. According to the *Gaṇapati Atharva,*[1] Gaṇeśa is the visible form of the realisation expressed in the words "thou verily in a visible form art that." The word "that" stands for the macrocosm, the word "thou" for man, the living being, the microcosm. By analogy, moreover, the word "that" stands for the non-manifest godhead; the word "thou" stands for its manifestation. In the conjoint image, the shapes interpenetrate. The limbs of man become elephantine in their proportions, the shape of the one component of the configuration being raised to the power of the other. For this reason the belly of Gaṇeśa is so large: Innumerable universes were born from it.[2]

The combined image of man and animal represents the realisation of the coherence of man and cosmos, and also, on a higher plane of reference, the coherence of this manifest cosmos with the stage beyond manifestation. Contracted in plastic form, the figures of man and animal cohere as one visual unit. The unity of the plastic form impresses on every Hindu the image in which he beholds and worships Gaṇeśa and makes those outside of Hinduism see the consistency and power of the image, even though the name Gaṇeśa, the Lord of hosts, the Ruler of all that can be counted, of all that has number and quantity, is unknown or meaningless to them.

Indian art neither depicts iconographic themes or mythical motives, nor does it illustrate allegories. It creates the coherent form of an empowered image, in which the transubstantiated, i.e., subtle body of man is coalesced with the shape of the animal; in which the figure of woman—conceived in proportions of the Mother-goddess—is entwined with a tree (Pl. 38). The shape of the woman and that of the tree remain distinct. Yet they are assimilated to one another, the arms resembling the stem of tree or creeper, the curves of the stem borrowed from those of the woman's body, both swaying in a coordinated rhythm, punctuated by shapes of flowers, garments, and ornaments, joints of the woman's body, and nodules of the plant. The woman leans against, touches, embraces, or climbs the tree in a visual image, frequently given verbal expression.

The Indian poet Kālidāsa[3] praises the creeper priyaṅgu that puts forth new blossom at the touch of a young woman. The aśoka tree flowers at the stroke of her foot, the tilaka at her glance, the kuravaka at her embrace, the nameru at her music, the karṇikāra

[1] Swāmī Hariharānand Sarasvatī, "The Greatness of Gaṇapati," *Journal of the Indian Society of Oriental Art* (1940), pp. 41–55.

[2] T. A. Gopinatha Rao, *Hindu Iconography,* I.1, p. 61.

[3] *Meghasandeśa,* N.S. ed. (1950), p. 60; cf. also *Karpuramañjarī,* I.27 and II.43.

at her dancing. There are further trees and creepers amongst the ten chosen species, for whose sake the Dohada rite is enacted. The Dohada rite is performed so that a certain tree may have flowers and fruits in abundance, even out of season, through a magic communication of the tree with the girl who, by the nearness and charm of her young body, by its movement, dance, and music, is believed to act on the tree. In the sculptured configuration (Pl. 38) this theme is enriched by the counterpoint of childlike figures at the base. They have heavy bellies, and, if they are female, their breasts are developed. These sprites, in their ungainly shapes, underline the progenitive symbolism. Their squat, grotesque playfulness contrasts with and sets off the perfect type of woman which the enchantress, the Śālabhañjikā, represents. Her natural beauty lies in her youth and, at the same time, in her destiny of motherhood, shown by the amplitude of her hips and the rotundities of her breasts, for the figure of woman in Indian sculpture has inherited some of its attributes from palaeolithic visions of the Great Mother.

The woman and tree configuration, in the consonance and intermingling of shapes, is an assurance of the felt correspondence and unity of human life and that of vegetation. It is symbolic of the calm of existence in a paradise when no gods had, as yet, ordained the laws by which this universe abides and strives; when "three ages before the gods, the plants were created" (*Ṛig Veda,* 10.97.1).

The third recurring configuration, composed of two separate figures, is the Mithuna, the couple in union (Pl. 17). Its lineage is as ancient as the combination of man and animal, or of woman and tree. A Mithuna is carved on the railing (about second century B.C.) of the Stūpa of the Saints (stūpa 2) in Sāñchī, where the ogress "Horseface," of human body and equine head, is seen roaming in a forest of toy-land trees and where, on another pillar, a woman is shown embracing her tree.

Mithuna, the "state of being a couple," is the plastic symbol of regained wholeness. "In the Beginning," says the *Bṛhadāraṇyaka Upaniṣad* (1.4.1–3), "was only the self in the shape of a person. Looking around, he saw nothing else but the self. He was afraid. Therefore, one who is alone is afraid. He then thought to himself: 'Since there is nothing else than myself, of what am I afraid?' Thereupon, his fear passed away. Assuredly, it is from a second that fear arises. He had no delight. Therefore, he who is alone has no delight. He desired a second. He became as large as a woman and a man in close embrace.—From that arose husband and wife.—He united with her."

Fear and loneliness prompt the Monad, the all encompassing principial Person, to desire a second; and by this desire, the Monad embraces what it desires and is as yet undivided. Then the principial person causes separation, in order to unite with the object of his desire. In this new united form, he is free from craving, free from fear. "As a man, closely embraced by a beloved woman, knows nothing more of a without or a within, so does the Person, when embraced by Foreseeing Knowledge (gnosis), the Self, know nothing more of a without or a within. This is his true form in which his desire is fulfilled, in which the Self is his desire, in which he is without desire, free from sorrow."[4]

The interlace of body and limbs of the couple in close embrace, in spellbound torsions of rapture, is also the symbol of the reunion of the Person and his Nature, of essence and substance as they are in principle and were in the beginning. Fear and desire have brought about the separation of the principle from itself. Desire unites him, the Person, with his nature. Desire, Kāma, cosmic Eros, separates and welds together the duality inherent in the Principle. The Person is united with his Nature, the "Foreseeing Knowledge" (prajñā) of Creation or of reintegration.

When visualised in terms of sculpture, the interlace of the limbs of the standing figures is based on difficult postures of sexual yoga, which intensify the embrace beyond even the possibilities of the physical act. India's religions know the figures of the Mithuna symbol by different names. In Mahāyāna Buddhism the principial actors are Gnosis (prajñā) and Means; to the Hindu they are Śiva and Gaurī, "embracing Śiva as the Mādhava creeper clasps the young Āmra tree with her bosom like a cluster of blossoms."[5]

The several symbols of correspondence and union are themselves interrelated. The young woman clasps and embraces the tree and thereby makes it flower in the Dohada rite. Woman in her principial aspect as Śakti, which is her power to manifest, clings to the Person, to Śiva, the Lord, in an embrace which enwraps him like a creeper (latāveṣṭitaka), and is like the movement of climbing a tree (vṛkṣādhirūḍhaka). In its plastic form, the union of the Principles is shown by joining or approaching to one another the shapes of man and woman, woman and plant, animal and man. By an inner logic of this process of unifying configuration, Gaṇapati, the elephant-headed Lord of hosts, embodiment of the correspondence of macrocosm and microcosm, is represented by the Shingon sect in Japan as Mithuna, in the dual form of Kangi-Ten.[6] The embrace of the standing, male and female, elephant-headed images conveys the union of the individual soul with the universal spirit, of the phenomenal and noumenal worlds. In the interlace of this configuration, the meaning of the Mithuna is reinforced by the embrace of the composite man-animal symbols.

The validity of the Mithuna symbol in Indian art is in the visualisation of the power which effects the union of the principles. Cosmic Eros welds the turgid, breath inflated, touching and rebounding shapes. Over and above the dramatic emblem of the Mithuna group, the symbol of reunion, there is an inner Mithuna in the figure of man as shown in Indian sculpture. Gaurī, the female principle, the nature and substance of all existence, embraces Śiva. Their union is known to be so close that the female principle (narī) is spoken of as Ardhāṅgī, as half of the body of the Lord. The total image of Śiva,

[4] *Br. Ār. Up.*, 4.3.21.
[5] Yogavāsiṣṭha, *Nirvāṇa-prakaraṇa*, 18.3.
[6] A. Getty, *Gaṇeśa* (Oxford, 1936), p. 84.

therefore, is that of the divine Hermaphrodite, Ardhanārīśvara, the "Lord whose half is woman," in the balance of the right side of his image which is male and the left which is female. But over and above this image of Śiva, which is one in the vertical dichotomy of the symbolism of right and left, most of the male figures of Indian sculpture carry in their adolescent shapes—the gods are conceived as eternally sixteen years old—lithesome feminine grace. Where the image of the goddess is that of potential motherhood and reflects that of the Great Mother, the image of a god is a reflection of the undivided principles as they were in the beginning in the primordial Person.

The figures of Indian sculpture are not descriptive of human appearance. They refer the human condition to the abiding concepts of the Great Mother and of the primordial Person in whom there is no division of the male and female principles. The mould of the images of Indian sculpture is made under the command of the cosmic Eros, but not all the Mithuna groups are its particular symbols. Not all of them reveal the secret of sexual union in divinity. Not all of them are hierophanies. Nor do all of them represent the sexual act as a theme swayed by the emotions and controlled by the mind bent on reintegration in the absolute. They illustrate the practice of sex as the ambivalent means toward the reunion with the Principle or towards the fall from all principle.

According to doctrines practised by Tantric sects, man's higher self could be gained through the experiences which would cause his downfall if he were unable to control his mind and body while undergoing them. Some thought that purgation of the self could be achieved by abuse of self, by excess for the sake of exceeding the condition of mortal man. In this quest, Rimbaud and the left-hand doctrine of the *Kulārṇava Tantra* have much in common. Others, again, recognised in desire the fetter which binds men to the objects of the senses and their pleasures. It was, therefore, necessary to be free from desire while tasting sensual pleasures. Voluptuousness without desire would be the paradoxical—and inadequate—attitude in this striving towards integration. Both these approaches, of overwhelming and of passionless passion, are illustrated in Mithuna groups of the temple walls. But there are others which express in their embrace one shared emotion (samarasa) in which enjoyment, compassion, and rapture seal the discovery of oneness in an eternal present by the conjoint pair (Pl. 14).

Though not all the Mithuna groups are charged with transcendental meaning, they have their place on the walls of the temple, where their effect is twofold. By appealing to one of man's primary drives, they hold the attention of the devotee, like the "beautiful women of the gods" (surasundarī) who are called "attractions" (ākarṣiṇī). Their images are stationed on the temple walls for the purpose of attracting the eye, the senses, and the mind of the devotee, so that he concentrates on them and becomes oblivious of all distraction. By contemplating their enthralling presence he is led into the temple. The "attractions" are the messengers (dūti) of the great goddess.

If the erotic scenes act as means of concentration, they effect detachment from all other concerns as does any object on which the mind intently dwells. If, on the other hand, the erotic scenes can be viewed with detachment, they are a confirmation that the devotee is not enslaved by desire, and his path is that of the hero (vīra) who masters his mind and body while in the midst of the adventure. By this test the devotee is brought near the ultimate purpose of the erotic scenes on the temple walls. They represent concrete rites in which the human eros is mastered as a means of obtaining supreme bliss (mahāsukha) of non-duality. In these rites the body is made to act free from the conditions and purpose imposed by nature on the union of the sexes. Seminal emission is arrested and the seed must not fall in the ritual embrace (*Gorakṣa Saṃhitā*, 61 f.). By this control of his body man surpasses the mortal condition and is godlike. The asceticism of voluptuousness rarifies the intensity of the embrace in its controlled abandon, when man, overcoming his mortal condition, is one with his Śakti or the creative power itself. But even this understanding does not fulfill the purpose of the Mithuna sculptures on the temple walls. If, however, over and above the significance of its theme, a Mithuna carving "can be enjoyed with a kind of enjoyment different from direct experience," that is, if intrinsically it is a work of art, then this enjoyment "is of the same order as the tasting of the Supreme Brahman."[7]

Though different in degree and dimension, aesthetic contemplation is one in kind with Mokṣa, the inner state of liberation from all contingencies of existence. A sculpture of a Mithuna whose subject matter ceases to be an object of direct, i.e., vicarious, enjoyment, and by its created form presents the experience of that enjoyment, the tension and rhythm of the inner transport as means and symbol of transcendence, has its place as much on the wall of the temple as in the domain of art.

In the Western view of art, nature and art are considered opposites, the one exceeding the other according to different points of view. Art itself is a record of the dialogue within the artist between him as creator of the work of art and nature as creation or *natura naturata*. The Indian sculptor in his concern with the sensible universe reaches out not for any particular aspect of the natural objects but for the process that makes them. The Indian sculptor sees in their shape nature at work and he records *natura naturans* according to his feeling and understanding of her mode of operation. The Mithuna symbol therefore has not only the shapes of man and woman as partners. The meaning of the symbol is expressed even more directly where the two who form a couple are entwined like serpents and are serpents (Pl. 21). Backed and surmounted by their cobra hoods, the Nāgas, denizens of the waters and symbols of the primordial generative power, are royal in their dignity and human in their tenderness. They meet and flow together, their serpent bodies interlace.

The different kinds of the Mithuna, the non-dual group of two, are carved in

[7] Raniero Gnoli, *The Aesthetic Experience according to Abhinava Gupta* (Rome, 1956), pp. 54–56.

the form and style of all the other sculptures which are on the walls of the same temple. The Mithuna figures and all the other figures of Indian sculpture are "prāṇa"-shaped; they are vessels of the life breath and movement; their "nakedness" is its plastic container, for the body of man is the visible sheath in which inheres the subtle prāṇa body. The subtle body being clothed in the physical body, all further covering would be redundant. The garments worn by the figures are reduced to nothing. They hug the body like invisible gloves. Their designs and folds are engraved on the body. Their hemlines are fastened to the body like thin, flexible wires. Only the scarves with their folds are massed as separate shapes. Where their volumes cling to the body they accentuate the swelling shapes and accompany their contours (Pl. 41). The small, and sometimes intricate, ornaments enhance by their contrast the large, melting planes of the sculptures. Drapery exists only by the side of the modelled body where it is massed as separate volume in a lower relief, rippling alongside the figure where it adds cascades of its own to festoons, loops, pendants, and belts (Pl. 38). Nothing is allowed to interfere with, everything is devised to enhance, the plasticity of the figures. Only in a late phase was the garment carved in its own volume, which encases that of the limbs (Pl. 51).

The texture of the naked body of sculpture is that of the stone or the metal of which the images are made. The fluidity and light-reflecting quality of the one material, the light absorbing surfaces of the other, hold the concrete and flowing volumes. Some of the stone sculptures were stained red (Pl. 8), others might have been finished with a thin coat of painted plaster.

Corresponding to the inner Mithuna in the figures of the gods is the inclusion of the tree or creeper in the figure of the "beauteous women of the gods" (surasundarī). In the Śālabhañjikā, the "woman and tree" motif, the stem of the tree often has the suppleness of a vine spreading into a flowering, foliated bower over the head of the goddess (Pl. 38). Or the stem is hidden behind the sinuous shape and lilt of the goddess. Even where the top of the tree is not shown, the sinuous shape and swaying stance (bhaṅga) of the goddess remain the same. She is then without cognisance, not a tree-woman, but an anonymous messenger communicating the message of her shape, in the flexions of the dance or holding a mirror, and stationed next to the images of the gods on the temple walls. Whatever her attitude, it is part of her being and expresses her nature. The images, whether of gods or goddesses, do not gesticulate; they are not conceived as actors in a cosmic drama, even when they are its protagonists (Pl. 8). They are embodiments of states of being and their concrete form.

Plastic form is the medium conveying images like that of the man-animal, the Mithuna, and the woman and tree, with their seen and felt correspondences. These in turn live in myths and are enacted as rites. Creation in visual and verbal terms stems from the same source and is active in the different media. While the mind thinks in images, the hand gives shape to the thought process together with its content, the thought-image, in a visual amalgam of motif and form, in which the total vision and awareness are embedded. The symbols in Indian sculpture are either primarily mind-made and taken up by the plastic stream, or they are altogether plastic. Mind-conceived symbols are the weapons, flowers, and other objects held in the hands of the statues and also the symbolic gestures (mudrā) of their hands. The wheel symbol, for example, which evokes the cycles of time, or the lotus with its open petals as a symbol of manifestation, or the sword that cleaves the cloud of ignorance are similes vested in objects, whereas the kinetic symbols, the gestures of the hands and the postures of the body, are expressive in themselves before they are represented in art. The raised hand, palm outwards (abhaya mudrā), commands and reassures; it allays the fear of existence, if the hand is that of divinity. When lowered, this palm in the gesture of giving a boon (varada mudrā) communicates the state of grace, free from anxiety, full of peace.

Whereas visual and verbal images and kinetic experiences enter the plastic flux, the visually plastic symbols issue from the plastic flux. Such a plastic symbol is the wave. The wave moves throughout the fields of Indian carving and takes the shape of the lotus rhizome. It rises and sinks in ever repeated rhythm, carrying lotus flowers and the fruits of all trees, and not only these but also the fruits of all actions. These are exemplified in the scenes which illustrate the stories of the former births of the Buddha.[8] These scenes are carved in the rising and falling of the wave. The wave in the shape of the lotus rhizome is a plastic equivalent of the theory of reincarnation. The autonomous dynamic of its form, in Buddhist art, carries the associated verbal meanings in an ever recurring pattern; ever new exemplifications from the former lives of the Buddha are drawn into the form of the wave. Or the wave is a mere abstract, raised line. In many later carvings it even has no tangible shape but is the principle of composition in panels replete with the plastic surge of nameless forms, their eddies and convolutions. They assume the likeness of leaves, animals, mythical figures, and drolleries. Even the major images themselves are variations of the underlying theme of plastic movement. Plastic movement itself has its symbol in the wave, either distinct in its own shape or pervasive in the entire composition, or else disguised as tree, as fluttering garment, or as bodily stance in the double and triple curve of sinuous bends (bhaṅga) of the figures. The wave is a form-giving symbol in contrast to the representational symbols, which in turn are carried by the plastic stream, for eye and mind to dwell on.

Another symbol in its own visual right is the Liṅga, the Sign of Śiva. The domed pillar shape of this central object of worship is phallic in effect and cosmic in its significance. It is full of generative power when beheld in its microcosmic reference. Macrocosmically it is at the same time the pillar of the universe and the sheath of manifesting deity. The rigour of its shape is translated into the motionless, unbending, upright

[8] As on the coping stone of the railing of Bhārhut. Cf. A. K. Coomaraswamy, *La Sculpture de Bharhut* (Paris, 1956), Pls. 41–51. L. Bachhofer, *Early Indian Sculpture,* Pls. 25–27.

stance of anthropomorphic images of the icon whether envisaged as god or goddess (Pls. 22, 24).

Plastic form itself is the symbolic form in which Indian sculpture visualises its contents. The contents are of two main categories. Plastic form as its own content throws forth the image of the wave and the pillar. These again are enriched by verbal images that are engulfed in the plasma of creative form.

The plastic form of the sculptures and the Indian mode of thinking in images, it has been shown already, are cognate creative phenomena. Moreover, the contents of the latter interpenetrate the former without dislocation. Indian sculpture never becomes peopled with figured allegories in a self-conscious exhibition of their circumscribed meaning, nor does meaning disrupt the form. These perils of Western art have no ground in Indian sculpture. Indian sculpture has fatal perils of its own, however. Death comes of stagnation of the plastic flow, when the inertia of the material looms in the emptied boundaries of a shape whose meaning remains in its name only. The verbal image then outlives the visual form as in the case of cult images. These continued to be made as props for religious concentration, a service which mere diagrams (yantra) render by their geometrical exactitude, without a claim to art.

Without its plastic quality, Indian sculpture recedes from the world of art into the limbo of instruments useful for, but not expressive of, a purpose. As an efficient tool, the image has its measure and proportion. Rules of proportionate measurement underlie the structure and guarantee the correctness on which depends the efficacy of the image (mūrti). They do not guarantee the quality of the image as work of art. The ancient imagers knew proportionate measurement to be the *sine qua non* of the craft, they also knew that none of the symbolical and magically effective numbers would make the sculpture artistically potent. They depended on their knowledge and put their trust in the creative moment of immediate intuition,[9] for this moment compulsively demands that its striking power be carried over to the rhythms and be converted into an order laid out in sacred numbers and the rules of proportionate measurement.

At the same time the importance of the objet trouvé must not be overlooked, for stones which are not worked on by man, but show the work of nature, are also worshipped. The fossilised ammonite, the Śālagrāma, is a symbol of Viṣṇu. Stones which have particular marks and are smoothed by the action of flowing water, the Bāṇaliṅgas, are symbols of Śiva. The sanctification of the objet trouvé—which is svayambhū or self-existent—is prompted by the discovery on the side of the devotee and by his acknowledgment, in these works of nature, of rhythms and patterns which also belong to art.

The vicarious use of natural form and art form accounts for the anonymity, in principle, of the Indian artist and craftsman. As vehicles of cosmic rhythms which they

[9] Cf. *Samarāṅgaṇasūtradhāra,* trans. in Stella Kramrisch, *The Hindu Temple,* p. 8.

communicate to their works, artists have fulfilled their function once the work is completed. Their connection with their work ends with the remuneration which they receive before the image is installed. No bond remains between the work and its maker. Once the work is accomplished, its power, released from the human carrier, dwells in the form, and its effect belongs to those who see and use this power. Because the purpose of a cult image of Viṣṇu is its actual efficacy in bringing the deity so close to the worshipper that he can serve and love it and even be oned with it, the accent, from the point of view of the user, is not on its quality of art as such but on its magic instrumentality.

The artist, on the other hand, conscious of this as well as his own instrumentality and his skill, withdraws from his work and remains anonymous. Occasionally he engraves on the base of the image his name and also that of his teacher, as statements of his responsibility and indebtedness. Although inscribed sculptures are few only, they occur at all ages—from the South gate of Sāñchī, in the early first century A.D., where Ānanda, the foreman of the artisans of the royal workshop, engraved his name[10] to "Amṛita, the wise, grateful, and good artist, pupil of Indranīlamaṇi," who signed his image of Sūrya, the Sun god, in Bengal, of the eleventh century.[11]

[10] Sir John Marshall and A. Foucher, *The Monuments of Sanchi,* II, Pl. XI.

[11] R. P. Chanda, *Mediaeval Indian Sculpture in the British Museum* (London, 1936), p. 66.

2

Plastic Form

INDIAN SCULPTURE, WHATEVER its material, has a unique plastic quality. The word plastic is here valid in its several applications. It implies that Indian sculpture is creative in the same sense as is the plastic force of nature, and that it is capable of producing continuous transformations. The modelling of Indian plastic art makes visible the creative principle active in its substance, and it is the mode of forming in this substance whatever subject the sculptor envisages. The images are based on the shapes of man, animals, and plants. Their lineaments are infused with the creative substance of sculpture and become concrete as works of art, replete with its livingness. In India life, at all times, has been known to be carried by the breath (prāṇa) and the pulsations of sap (rasa) throughout the organism. It is on these principles of breath and sap that Indian plastic art is modelled. Its recognisable shapes appear filled with these shaping contents. The flux and pulsations of life shape, and are contained in, their boundaries. They define the particular images, whether these resemble the figure of man, animal, or plant used separately, or in their configurations as couple in union, man-animal, or woman-plant. The images are formed in an awareness of the spirit or breath of life, of its flux and pulsations, by the creative command under which the artist works. Form is the result of the rhythm of this activity.

The configurations of Indian sculpture are based on what the eye sees, but proceed beyond empirical truth to express the metaphysical. Mortal man, limited in action, has only two arms and hands; but an Indian image of divinity may have many times that number to show the divine acts in all the directions of space throughout the cosmos. The pliable plastic form in which the arms proliferate sculpturally is consistent in itself, yet may appear paradoxical when thought of outside the creative mould in which the multiple arms and hands are cast as symbols. These and many more configurations of Indian sculpture have, in fact, no reality other than in states of inner awareness and, hence, in form. Because they have no physical existence in nature, their structure is of an order different from that of things seen outside art. Inner affinities relate their shapes; they coalesce under the tension of contrasts and proliferate through the plasma of which they are formed. In it they are precipitated and take shape. Their context has the logic and fluency of the plastic medium in which they are conceived and by which they are borne and sustained. It is their substance and, at the same time, the frame in which they are moulded. Ontologically, they are plastic; visually, they are the form in which the breath and flux of life shape and fill the protagonists of myths and their symbols.

The plastic form of Indian sculpture is its creative idiom, the locus of the sculptor's immediate intuition, wherein he executes the command of his vision. It is the primal substance of his art. Generation after generation of sculptors shared in it. Their work exists to this day in stone and metal, whereas most of it, created in clay, wood, ivory, and other less durable materials, has perished.

The primal substance received the changing impresses of the surroundings, of the place and homeland of the sculptor, and recorded the changing pressures of history.

The impresses and pressures of the primal substance produced the styles in which the schools of Indian sculpture handed down the plastic form. While the local schools canalised the flow of the plastic substance, its bed, in the end, constricted with the silt made of the consciously practised norms and canons of the school. Where the norms, which were contrived as safeguards of the plastic substance, became its fetters, Indian sculpture lost its plastic quality.

The plastic quality of Indian sculpture is the created, visual counterpart to an awareness of the body as a receptacle filled with breath and the pulsations of life. The physique of the body is the concern of the science of medicine, not of art. Nor is it primarily the concern of Yoga discipline, the specific and highly elaborated Indian technique which aims at mastery of the body by harnessing its vitality according to the principles felt and known to animate the mortal frame. According to Yoga doctrine, thousands of channels (nāḍī) carry the life movement, the "vital air" (prāṇa), throughout the living body. They were imagined as subtle currents originating in assumed and experienced centres in the abdomen and heart,[12] leading to the openings of the body, to the suture of the skull, to eyes and ears, to the other organs of sense, and to those of sex. Prāṇa is in the heart and pervades the entire body. In the pulsation of the vital airs, life itself (jīva) throbs against the walls of the body[13] and makes the skin taut and resilient with its movement. This inner sensation of pulsating life, breathing its spirit to the tips of the fingers, and into every movement and mien, is captured in the plastic quality of Indian sculpture. Indian sculptural form, then, is neither a record of the appearance nor of the structure of the body. It aims rather to render the inner experience and awareness of life in the body, the life which sustains the shape of the body and keeps it flexible, expanding and receding with the movement of breath and the pulsations of sap.

The "vital breath" (prāṇa) is felt to be the sap and essence (rasa) of the body in

[12] *Bṛhadāraṇyaka Upaniṣad,* 2.1.19.
[13] *Yoga Cūḍāmanyupaniṣad,* 14–31.

all its limbs.[14] Prāṇa, the essence itself of the sap of life, and the vehicle of the life movement permeating the body, communicates its movement to all the vital currents within the body. In sculpture, this life-carrying agent is the core of the modelling. Rasa is its effect. The meanings of the word rasa include: sap, taste, and the object of taste, delight. Rasa constitutes the aesthetic experience of Indian sculpture as its direct sensual impact. The connoisseur is rasajña, one who knows rasa.[15] The "tasting of rasa" (rasāsvāda) corresponds to the art of criticism.

The body, as given form by Indian sculpture, is the shape of the inner experience of its life. The sculpture does not depict the concrete, gross (sthūla) physique as perceived and interpreted, but shows the subtle (sūkṣma) reality of life as felt in and through the body. The body of man in Indian sculpture is transubstantiated, quick with life, unhampered by gravity or stress, an organized volume of vital presence.

The physical shape of man in India favors this form—the bony frame and muscular development generally being comparatively slight, and the skin smooth. Moreover, the physiognomy of every regional type impresses its mould on the countenance of the sculptures. The divine visage confronts the worshipper in the cast of his own features, and those of the people around him, perfected in an ideal norm. The gods, in their stone and metal images, remind the worshippers of their own perfectibility, in accordance with their own natures.

Technically, Indian sculpture is mainly in relief and is part of a larger, monumental context, as are the railing posts or casing slabs of a Stūpa, the monument of Nirvāṇa—and of the Buddhist doctrine—or the carved temple walls. The surge of the plastic form conditions the type of the relief. The figures appear as though embossed on a flat ground, and this is partly true even when the relief is very low (Pl. 1, about first century B.C.). The deceptively primitive look of the flat expanses within the body of this figure, which is rounded off ever so little towards the outlines, is betrayed by the fuller modelling and higher relief of the head of the worshipper, represented on a railing post from Bhuvaneshvar, Orissa. In other carvings of some early monuments, such as those from Jaggayyapeta in the Āndhradeśa,[16] the three-dimensionality of the female figures, carved in the lowest relief, is presented in a tour de force of modelling-in-miniature. This is combined with foreshortenings which belong to a fully evolved plastic style. The technical restraint in the surface of three-dimensional values in the stone reliefs of this and other Buddhist monuments of the same period would seem to be the result of infiltrations of linear idioms belonging to tribal art into the full and more differentiated modelling of an established tradition. Of this ancient tradition, however, very little is known to have

[14] *Bṛhadāraṇyaka Upaniṣad,* 1.3.8 and 19.
[15] *Uttararāmacarita,* 2.22.
[16] H. Zimmer, *The Art of Indian Asia,* Pl. 37.

survived from the centuries prior to the third century B.C., that is, from the ages following the art of the proto-Indian city civilization (Harappa) after the second millennium B.C.

When Indian stone sculpture re-emerges in the third century B.C., it is seen full fledged in its own plastic form in the elephant cut out of the rock in Dhauli, Orissa. From then on, but for the exceptions and compromises in the earliest Buddhist monuments, the figures of Indian stone sculpture appear on their ground as if driven forward by a power indwelling in the stone which meets the sculptor's tools and is defined by them. Metal sculpture, cast in a "lost wax" process, is in the round. It shows the interplay of plastic volumes bonded in space by flowing contours. In much of the well-turned limbs and in much of the intricate decor of the stone carvings and metal sculptures, the innumerable and perished sculptures in clay, wood, ivory, and precious stones have left their traces.

3

The "Subtle Body" in Sculpture

THE FIGURES OF Indian sculpture are forms of experiences and realisations within the human body. The body is their place of reference and its shape their outer limit. The figures of Indian sculpture are plastic vessels filled with a potent continuum in recognisable bodily shapes. These vessel shapes, carved in stone or cast in metal, whether globular or pearlike, cylindrical or conical, merge into one another. The transitions from spherical to elongated volumes are similar to but richer than those of the forms of pottery. Their surface appears dilated by an inner movement which swells and sustains the figures of Indian sculpture whether they are shown immobilized in standing and seated postures or bending in torsions around their axis. This inner movement pervades the whole figure, from finger tips to toe, and keeps its surface taut, brimful as it is with the surging continuum. The nature of this continuum is known to the sculptor by direct experience and it is made visible in the form of sculpture. It is a knowledge of and within his own body which he conveys to the convex confines of his figures. By giving form to it he hypostasises the pervasive experience of being alive, of being sustained by the rhythmic pulsations of the sap of life and by breath. Spontaneously conscious of the flux of life within his own body, he creates his figures as vessels of the life movement. This is his primary concern. It is not the only one, for the consciousness which affirms the life movement can also turn against it while being sustained by it.

The figures of Indian sculpture are first of all the form of the fact of being alive. Since life is experienced within the whole body, including its surface, the volume and planes of sculpture are disposed so as to contain and convey this fact. It is not the appearance of the body to which the Indian sculptor gives form; it is not the knowledge of the eye alone which guides him. He does not primarily observe and transcribe what he sees or remembers. Rather, he uses direct observation and memory image to support the knowledge of life which he feels in his own body. He gives form to life as he feels it in the closed unit of his body. Because he forms life, he does not portray any human figure. Life is greater than any of its shapes or carriers. While basing his sculptures on the appearance of man, he transmutes and transcends appearance. Each carved figure is a vehicle of life itself, holding in its volume the weightless power of breath and in its outlines the tangible flux of its sap.

The figures of Indian sculpture are based primarily on a reality which is not seen but felt. Their object is not given outwardly. It exists inwardly. It is not abstracted and mind born; it is sensorily experienced. It does not become a concept but is made form directly. Indian sculpture is sensuous irrespective of its subject and even counter to its subject. However austere the theme is—as the images of the Jain Saviours (Tīrthankara) —or the Yantra-like geometry and the symbolism of signs (lakṣaṇa) of a Buddha image, the sculptural form is suffused with life experienced in the movement of the sap that fills the volume of the body which is sustained by breath.

Neither the muscular beauty and structure of the male body nor the sensual delight in the texture and shape of the female body activates the form which Indian sculpture has given to its figures. Their proportions and rhythms are primarily a part not of the transformed physical and visible reality of the body but of its transformed subtle and felt reality. The data given to the Indian sculptor are first of all those which are felt within his own body, the breath, the palpitation of the heart, the pulsation of the blood. The entire surface of his skin is breathing and tingling with warmth. In this experience of the body the skin is felt to be a living limit against the "ocean of the air" that touches it on all sides and meets the movement of the breath on the bounding tissue. Sky-clad (śvetāmbara) is a term which designates the naked Jaina ascetics. But the wide bell of the sky is the cloak under which each being exists in its nakedness. Indian sculpture, rich in ornaments and raiments, has known at all times how not to conceal the naked body with its smooth, breathing, palpitating skin. The figures of Indian sculpture have a tactile quality and seem to rebound by merely being looked at. The living vessel of the body is full of inner movement which holds its own against and communicates with that of the ocean of the air outside it, all over its surface, the skin. Transformed in sculpture this experience demands the taut, resilient planes where body and limbs offer their flowing, unbroken contours.

Rarely in Indian sculpture is the skin felt to be stretched over muscles and bones and to cover the carnal and mortal nature of the body. The osseous frame is hardly seen in Indian sculpture. The figures do not appear to be supported by it—and yet the firmly knit framework of bones is a postulate which the Jains set up for the body of their saviours.[17] The images of these saviours (Tīrthankara), however, stand firm like pillars and sit erect on the broad basic triangle of their interlocked legs. The firmness of the osseous framework is translated into a configuration of body parts solid in the interplay of compact, rounded, and near geometrical shapes in which the inner flux of life seems congealed and the breath arrested (p. 94).

The flux of life and the breath of life are the core on which the sinuosities of Indian sculpture are modelled. They enhance the less regular forms of nature, though their harmony is not derived from the appearance of the latter nor from their known

[17] *Triṣaṣṭiśālakāpuruṣacaritra, Gaekwad Oriental Series,* 51, trans. Johnson, p. 94.

structure, but from the directly experienced life that dwells in them and sustains them. The sculptures are its formal statement, each of their parts contributing its recognisable shape and name to the whole.

The living flow of the life sap has its visual equivalent in a viscous quality of form as if the plastic substance were poured into a vessel or mould. This mould is congruous with the skin-tight sculptural surface. It fits and follows the slow and steady flux and puts on record tensions and tremors as they are carried along. At no time during its known historical course, nor in its proto-Indian phase (Harappa, third millenium B.C.), were the leading schools of Indian sculpture without it. The rock-cut figure of the elephant in Dhauli, Orissa (mid third century B.C.), emerging from a hill, is a bounteous shape whose animality is proffered with a calm authority vested in the modelled mass. But whether the figure is that of an animal or, far more frequently, that of man, whether it is carved in stone or cast in metal, whether it is in the round or in the lowest relief (Pl. 1), its flowing contours and the expanding modelling are replete with the surge and spread of plastic mass. Like the sap of a plant, it keeps erect the shape which it fills. There is no inducement to refer the upright stance of the figure to its bony scaffold or to any muscular exertion which would counteract the pull of gravity. Though the figure is articulate in its joints, these are accentuated zones which allow for a change of direction and mediate between them; nor does the unity of the modelled expanse of the figure allow the neck to isolate the head and claim for itself special attention. A broad, short neck connects head and body; the modelling of the latter conveys as much of the content of the figure as "blossoms forth" (unmīl) and is laid out in the face. The masklike countenance in early Indian sculpture is as much in keeping with the body below as is the subtle, acutely differentiated visage of the figures after the fourth century with the rarefied tensions of curved planes and body contour.

In Indian sculpture there is no dichotomy between the head as seat of the intellect and spirit and the body with its sensual drives and responses. Most of the sense organs are located in the head and the entire body is animated by respiration, in which the spirit abides and is known to have its centre in the cavity of the heart (hṛd-ākāśa). Within the length of the body, moreover, to the crown of the head, subtle centres (cakra) are introspectively known in yoga-states. From the root centre, seventy-two thousand subtle currents pervade the entire living being.

The dichotomy of spirit and body is nonexistent in the figures created by Indian sculpture. The sensitivity and expressiveness of the face do not exceed those of the hand. The tips of the fingers are curved as delicately and knowingly as the lips. In this respect, a Buddha image of the sixth century from Sārnāth compares with any image of Śiva or Viṣṇu from Khajurāho of the eleventh century, and any of these gods compare with the goddesses whose countless images adorn the walls of the temples. The plasticity of all these figures has a common denominator, but its two main factors differ in quantity.

The two main factors of Indian plasticity are the qualities within the "subtle body" (sūkṣma śarīra) which belong to the flux and sap of life and those which are carried by the breath. The former makes the vitality of the sculptures. This factor is vegetative and aqueous by extraction. The wave is its symbol. The sinuous, gliding convexities of the sculptures carry it nowhere as fully as in the female figures of the temple walls. But it is more ancient than these carvings. In the early, narrative reliefs of the centuries around the beginning of the Christian era, the sinuous flux was the main compositional movement. Its carriers, whether of male or female shape, yielded to its course with tubelike limbs swaying with and traversed by the movement which at one and the same time placed and shaped the figures. In these early, narrative reliefs executed under Buddhist patronage, reliefs like those from Bhārhut and other sites in mid-India, Orissa (Pl. 1) and the northeastern Deccan, the plastic context is truly that of Saṃsāra. The word Saṃsāra denotes the life of this world and literally means a "flowing together" of the currents that motivate and sustain existence. The flux of life is felt in all living, moving shapes. They share in it in this world, as the figures in the reliefs are part of and borne by it. The flowing compositional movement is the spontaneous cadence of form; the tubelike limbs of the figures are its ducts. From this flowing ground of communicating shapes, the art of later centuries extracts its pure inflections. The female figures, the images of the goddess, are wreathed in them. They exalt life in its flowing movement.

The female figures, the images of the goddess, are not "an undisguised exaltation of physical desire." Its heat does not consume or burn unquenched; it is ingrained in the flux of life. Its waves wash away itch and torment. Desirable like fruits and shaped like fruits are the bodies and limbs of the goddess, images of potential motherhood, fulfilled in their promise, whose curving hips billow towards spheres which are breasts of more than human capacity. These widely spaced globes raise the figure's centre of gravity from its natural place, the navel, to near shoulder height. It is from there that the body appears suspended, as if weightless in the wide, complementary arcs of hip and chest. If their surge is continued, in a cherished often repeated posture (tribhaṅga), the raised arm frames the head and leads back the undulating movement of the figure to its starting point in the middle of the body, the waist and hip-belt. At this centre of bodily flexion and torsion the modelling is rich in tension and intimate, for embedded in it is the place of the origin of life, the small, deep pit of the navel. From this pivotal point, the burgeoning shapes of the goddesses swell forth in gyrations around the axis of the body. The favourite posture of the female figure in Indian sculpture, the tribhaṅga—the triple bend comprising an "enhanchement" on one side, the corresponding lateral thrust of the opposite shoulder, and the balancing bend of the head in the direction opposite to that of the shoulder—is centred in this zone. The supporting leg extends the curvaceous movement downward, as the raised arm prolongs it upward. The "triple bend" is a movement in situ. It is not a stance as is the Greek contrapost where the weight of the body rests on the supporting leg. The Greek contrapost, a stance in which the pull of gravity is counteracted by muscular exertion, corresponds to an architectural concept of weight and support stated in Greek architecture in terms of columns and architrave. No such architectural correspondence is valid in any of the attitudes of the figures of Indian sculpture. If an Indian goddess is shown standing straight and pillarlike (sama-pada-sthānaka [Pl. 22]), this is the exception when she, like the cult images of the great gods, is an embodiment of the "pillar of the universe." This pillar symbol supports the vault of the sky, which has no physical weight. Incorporating the world pillar, the image in the likeness of man or woman, unlike the Greek Kore or Caryatid, is divested of weight.

In their general posture, the figures of the goddesses gyrate around their vertical axis, sinuous in their interlacing profiles. These are taut by a double movement: one is the flux itself which engenders the plasticity of the shape whose profiles they are; the other is their interlace in space. The former is that of the subtle plastic medium poured into the body-shape so that its form burgeons forth luscious and replete with sap. Swelled by it, body and limbs appear self-supporting without corporeal weight, filled with creative dynamism that has flown into and expanded the form. The form has swelled and ripened into roundness from within. Its rotundities glide and surge serpentwise and fruitlike; they are taut and controlled limits of the subtle substance. Their shapes approximate those of vessels; their profiles approach the perfection of parabolic curves and circles.

The creative dynamism by which the body in its parts and their transitions are turned into shape informs the line of their profiles and guides the bodily postures traced and composed in space (Pl. 38). Their rhythms conform with those of the shapes themselves of the sculptured body. The curve and rhythm of an arm raised above and behind the head are consonant with the outline of the hip. The curve of physical movement as performed in space has its measure determined by that of the bounding curves of the volumes of the body. The curves bounding the volumes of a figure and the curves traversing the space which the figure fills by the movement of its posture are similar. Their likeness springs from the creative dynamism of "subtle substance" that fills and shapes the figure.

Where the goddesses are accompanied by the small figures of attendants (gaṇa [Pl. 38]), these dwarfed female or male bodies are visualisations of the boundless capacity of the plastic medium congealing into shape when the conjoint controls of bodily discipline and of an ideal of bodily perfection are removed. The sagging bulges of the female gnome-shape contrast with the firm profiles of the goddess, and the flexed continuity of the volumes of either of those figures "in movement" is enhanced by their contrast with the abrupt juxtaposition of the near geometrical volumes of the musical instrument (vīṇā). Upheld as it is by the Gaṇa, the instrument acts as a measuring rod between abundance and excess of plastic substance welling forth in the female shapes.

In all the female figures, the impact of the plastic substance is strongest between breasts and hips, between the high centre of gravity and the centre of movement. The breast orbs are proffered from the chest. They remain unforeshortened by the posture of the figure. They are symbols of her being, vessels of her plenitude, emblems which she carries. Their volumes, symmetrically sent forward into space, balance that of the head.

The head is the apex of the triangle of these volumes full of meaning. This is laid out in the divine countenance where the vault of the forehead holds the tension of the brows, shading the meditative eye, and the sharp ridge of the nose leads to the tenderness of lips full of sensuous knowledge (Pls. 44, 23). In these features the plastic content of the face comes to the surface, creating a visage whose physiognomy is transmuted into a landscape of the intellect and the emotions. The features are carried by the inner, plastic life movement; their accents rise with calm authority. They seal the meaning of the face, the place where the body exposes the reason for its existence. The face is guarded and enclosed by coiffure, crown, and ornaments. Wreathed by the minutiae of their diverse shapes, the face, underscored by the ring of the neck, is linked to the expanse of the body. The expanse of the chest of the female figures is a place for the ornaments to rest (Pls. 38, 44). Plastically, it is the least alive surface of the female body in Indian sculpture, a plane of transition from the attributes of the goddess as the Great Mother to her self-revelation in the lineament of her face.

The chest, however, is the most emphatically modelled part of the body of the gods in Indian sculpture[18] and the pre-eminent part of the torso whose highly differentiated unit extends from the exaggerated width of the shoulders to the hips. The distention of the shoulders and the transition into the arms resemble a powerful horizontal bar by which the length of the body is held up, and its weight appears lifted from the feet, though the soles rest on the ground (Pl. 9). The centre of gravity in the male figure of Indian sculpture is in the expanse of the broad shoulders and the chest. It is from there that the rest of the standing figure is lowered onto the ground. The ground is the pericarp of a lotus flower, symbol of total manifestation and ground of existence. It supports the presence of divinity which does not weigh on it (Pls. 9, 19). The broad-shouldered, well-endowed figures of the gods are free from gravity as are those of the goddesses; they too are self-supporting and effortless. In the fullness of their splendour they confront the devotee as if with bated breath. It fills the expanse of their shoulders and chest.

The images of the gods, whatever be their stance—straight as a pillar or slightly bent, standing or seated, or lying—are always shown full of the breath which expands their chest and seems arrested in the powerful volume of their bodies (Pls. 9, 12, 19, 24,

[18] The cult images are meant to be seen from the front. Images of attendant figures are occasionally shown in profile or back view.

26). The image appears to float because it is filled with breath. If the breath could be retained within the mortal body, it would not die. This knowledge was given practical effect in Yoga, which developed the most thorough discipline and efficient technique for mastering the breath in order to overcome the mortal condition. By regulating the rhythm of respiration (prāṇāyāma) and slowing it down by holding the breath beyond average human endurance, a waking state as calm as sleep was attained, a state replete with power and a feeling of weightlessness which testified the Yogin's detachment from the physical contingencies of existence and transferred him into the state of unconditional being while within his body. This realisation within the body by a mastery of breath fills its confines with the power of breath, held, arrested so that it cannot flee. Its realised permanence pervades a body of power, the yoga-body (yoga-deha; Pl. 24).[19] The yoga body penetrates the living body, and dilates it from the centre of being.

Quickened by and abiding in this state of power the yoga body is created in sculpture. The yoga body also like the body of flowing life is a mode of the subtle body. The physical body (sthūla śarīra) has its modes of waking and sleeping. They belong to it from the beginning and modify its appearance in the waking or the sleeping states. The subtle and invisible body (sūkṣma śarīra) is formed by the inner awareness of the flowing movement of life within the confines of the physical body. This awareness is spontaneously given form in Indian sculpture. This form is the basic form of Indian sculpture. It is the form of fluidity which gives its quality to the modelling.

The inner awareness of breath also constitutes the subtle body. These two modes of awareness are as inseparable and distinct as are the waking and the sleeping states of the physical body. But the body of breath is not the spontaneous form of the awareness of breathing. It is the form of breath arrested. This yoga body is not the form of an inner awareness of life as it is spontaneously experienced. Rather it is the form of a special awareness which is induced by methodical effort, by a deliberate striving for the cessation of flux and transitoriness for a state of rest in undiminished power. This state is realised inwardly by suspending the breath so that its full volume stays within the walls of the body.

The yoga body is a willed form of the subtle body. Its proportions are based on a canon of mathematical correspondences, a norm of ideal appearance which is the scaffold for the yoga body modelled on and upheld by breath. Breath dilates the chest (Pls. 9, 12) and back (Pl. 43) in surging arcs of its own. They wing towards the shoulders, their tensions enhanced by the pulsating life sap which beats against the walls indwelt by breath. The expanse of the torso with its triangle linking the modelling of the breasts and around the navel is as plastically expressive and formally fulfilled as the facial triangle of eyes and mouth (Pls. 12, 19, 26). The body, upheld and dilated by breath, is the inspired creation of Indian sculpture from the seventh to the thirteenth century.

[19] *Yogabīja,* 49; see S. Dasgupta, *Obscure Religious Cults* (Calcutta, 1946), pp. 252, 253.

The spiritual physiognomy of Indian sculpture matured slowly. In the early phases (Pl. 1) the body was a vessel of the life sap, defined by a more or less abbreviated generalisation of its appearance. By the second century (Amarāvatī) the male body began to acquire a heroic cast—the great width of shoulders, the breath-inflated, articulate chest, the disciplined abdominal region narrowed and enlivened by a modelling as sensitive as that of the chest.[20] In the major and mainly Buddhist images of the Gupta age (fourth century to ca. 600) the austere power of the yoga body holds in its thrall the flux and pulsations of the subtle body of vegetative life. After that, the heroic, pneumatic yoga body becomes congruous with the form of the subtle body of vegetative life. Their visual identity would seem a paradox, for the state of arrested breath means the conquest of mortality, cessation of the flux of life. But Prakṛti, the primordial matrix, is not annihilated. By controlling the movement of breathing and making it rhythmical, her flowing bounty is freed from deforming latencies which accrue from the conditions of life. It is this conditioning by life that wastes away in time, the hardening or weakening of its vessel, and the accumulation of residual matter which Yoga knows how to eliminate and annihilate. Physically the Yogin continues to live in his body during and after the ultimate realisation of samādhi, for which his discipline with ever increasing wisdom and power has prepared him. In sculpture, the created form of the subtle body with its pulsating vegetative quality and flowing rhythm subsists when this form is inflated by the power of breath. The subtle body of flowing movement is imaged pre-eminently in the lineaments of the goddesses with their curves of fulfillment. In the awareness of their flux is the experience of ripening and wholeness.

Yoga as a discipline of the body is devised primarily for the male body. Its all-important technique is the regulation and retention of breath. The perfection of the yoga body in art is primarily that of the body of the gods (cf. Vyāsa's commentary on Patañjali, *Yogasūtra,* III.26), who like the yogins are above the human condition. The goddesses, being equal in status to the gods, participate in their images in the form of the yoga body. Conversely, the images of the gods are not only permeated by the principle of fluidity conveyed by their modelling, but they also have assimilated typically female curves. With rounded hips and nascent breasts their images have taken into themselves the female element (Pls. 9, 12, 19, 41). While these are images of particular gods (Pls. 9, 19) they portray the monadic phase, prior to dichotomy and the differentiation of male and female. The image of Śiva-Ardhanārīśvara is an iconographic rationalisation of the divine form of the gods in Indian sculpture. In their images the flux of life within the confines of the body is steeped in the power of the spirit of which the breath is the agent. The flux of life pervaded and controlled by the power of the breath and the spirit is the inextricable subtle substance of which the bodies of the gods are modelled. The ground swell of

[20] In Northern India of the second and third centuries the physical bulk of the Yakṣa statues became gradually translated into the breath-inflated Yoga body.

their shape communicates this deep power in—and over—breath. Their smooth, clear surfaces offer themselves to be seen and touched but their sensuousness is more than skin deep. It wells up from their core.

Representational visual art in the West relies on the eye, on an approach from the outside towards the object which is seen. The beating heart, the respiration, and the neuro-vegetative system are not seen. Indian sculpture relies on life as it is felt within the body and on realisations that transcend life although their locus is the body. Indian sculpture takes creative cognisance of all the levels of inner, bodily awareness. The eye of the sculptor takes stock of the living shape as the outer limit and receptacle of the invisible, though felt, mysterious mechanism and fabric whose movement and texture are palpable. The tactile quality of Indian sculpture results from a sensorial verification and identification of the living, sustaining reality. It is not only the sculptor who so uses his sense of touch. By the rite of Nyāsa the worshipper touches the image which he worships as concrete symbol and he touches his own body at definite spots, awakening his consciousness to the presence of divinity at those parts of the body.

In his creative spontaneity the sculptor forms the body as the vessel of the flux and palpitations of life. His work is in praise of life, in praise of the living body, the seat of life, of consciousness and of the effort of consciousness to master and transcend life. This effort goes to the source. Going from within the current to the source means a going counter to the current. Where the current is that of life itself going to the source reaches the end of the current. In this supreme effort of consciousness the movement of breath is arrested at will by means of prāṇāyāma. By this discipline the yogin is in possession of the principle of life, the breath. He "holds" the breath for a period beyond untrained endurance, neither inhaling nor exhaling, wrapt in the consciousness of a deathless dying—while slowly and calmly life flows on. He reaches the source beyond life as he holds and immobilises the breath. He has withdrawn from life while living, has overcome mortality. He is liberated and godlike. He has "called into being out of this body another body of the mind's creation (rūpiṃ manomayam) with transcendental faculties (abhinindriyam)."[21]

This power of the Yogin arises in the artist when he evokes the presence of deity. He identifies himself with its reality inwardly seen and felt and makes the concrete work of art its image. Its tangible presence is vested in a transubstantiated form, that of the yoga body, in which the undulations of the subtle body of flowing life are rarefied.

The seemingly weightless yoga body of the images of Indian sculpture is bounded by convex walls with clear-cut profiles in front and side views. In the later phases (eleventh-twelfth centuries) in an excess of breath-inflated power, the vaulting volumes of the body shown in back view meet in a forward thrust of movement on a concave curve—which is the spine—strained to breaking point (Pl. 43). At this phase the naked yoga

[21] *Majjhima-Nikāya,* 3.7: *Dialogues of the Buddha,* II.17 (trans. Chalmers).

body is shown pressing against the girdles by which it is clasped and the scarves by which it is tied (Pls. 43, 41). They help to keep its power within its confines.

The yoga body, an acquired, induced state of realisation and a psychophysical reality, is given form in the sculptures of the gods and goddesses who have no other body. The body of flowing life is the form of a spontaneous awareness by introverted attention to the sap as nature drives, regulates, and holds it within the living being. The yoga body of arrested breath is the form of a special yet immediate awareness by introverted attention to breath controlled by will and caught against nature, arrested within the living being. The body of flowing life surges and ebbs in its ever renewed rhythms. They are held in suspense when the yoga body has pervaded them. The body of flowing life is the yielding, feminine, time-bound body. The yoga body is the body of will by which the former is overcome; it defies and absorbs time, whose flux it binds to its expanse. Both these "bodies" coincide and fill the receptacle of sculptural form.

The inner experience of the body of flowing life and of the yoga body is impressed from within on the palpable modelling of the figures, so that they appear exposed to view, naked, although richly bejewelled and wearing various garments (Pls. 3, 38, 53). The folded scarves and draped loincloths, however, are made incorporeal by the contact of these subtle bodies. Their folds leave their traces on the surging volumes either in curves and rippling lines which enhance the modelled smoothness of the body by their phantom fabric or massed as compact zones and girdles. Chest and hips are bound by them, also the roundness of the limbs (Pls. 9, 12, 52, 57), and they encircle the head (Pls. 10, 20, 23). These devices tie, accentuate, separate, and connect the swelling volume. Their definition measures its impact, their elaboration offsets, answers, and relieves the expanse of its vaulting planes.

4

The Image

THE SANSKRIT WORD for image is Mūrti. Mūrti means something concrete, of definite shape and fixed measurement—an embodiment. When the completed work has left the hand of the sculptor and is consecrated, when the priest by a symbolic rite (prāṇa pratiṣṭhita) invests it with the breath of life, or divinity, which its shape embodies, the image becomes a Mūrti. Thus, Mūrti denotes the final stage by which an image becomes concretely real. Altogether realised and bodily present as a visual integer, it is now fit to be worshipped as the locus in which the spirit is manifest.

The concrete reality of the image or work of art creatively formed, and in which ritually the deity is established, exists in its own sphere where its power is supreme and its effect undisturbed. This place is the innermost sanctuary of the temple. There the image or symbol is beheld, in the rite of "seeing" (darśana), in its total effect and meaning. The power established within the image in the innermost sanctuary is delegated also to its "lateral images" which are the pārśvadevatās enshrined in niches in the thickness of the outer temple walls, in the main directions of space (Pl. 9). The pārśvadevatās are flanked by the sculptures of the lesser gods.

The worshipper goes to a temple to see the house and body of God. This "seeing" (darśana) bestows grace. It is regulated by a mode of approach, a preparation prescribed by the plan of the temple itself. Darśana is the act of seeing with complete understanding of the thing seen. It is an induced "intuition" which has its ritual or practical method. Darśana, the seeing approach, is also the name for the various methods of cognising truth. These "methods" are the Indian systems of philosophy.

Mūrti, the concrete form, requires Darśana, the seeing awareness, achieved by the rites of approach (adhigamana and pradakṣiṇā). Adhigamana is the approach in a straight line towards the object of contemplation. The object appears in front view. From a distance it is seen as one plane, the target on which eye and mind are focussed. Pradakṣiṇā is a walking around the object of contemplation; it offers all its profiles to the devotee, addresses itself to him as sculpture.

The image or symbol of the deity enshrined in the temple is placed on a pedestal in the middle of the innermost sanctuary which is a small, square chamber. If the symbol has the shape of the Liṅga, this "sign" of Śiva rises from the centre of the sanctuary. The cylindrical shape of the Liṅga is complete in itself, but its meaning is made explicit where four of its faces are carved in relief on its sides facing East, West, North, and South (Pl. 49). The Liṅga is sculptured completely in the round. When seen from the front, the Liṅga is framed by the elaborately carved, rectangular doorway of the sanctuary. Thus the Liṅga, beheld in the warm glow of oil lamps, is the focus of a framed composition which has its own space and depth and is filled by a luminous chiaroscuro.

In the temples of gods other than Śiva, the image is figured forth in lineaments which have the shape of man. The icon (Pls. 22, 24) in the middle axis of the sanctuary is seen in the door frame, an illumined apparition, when approached in one straight line from the entrance of the shrine. The icon has the shape of a stele, whose main figure, even though carved almost, and in part wholly, in the round, projects from the lower relief of the carvings of the slab. The total effect is that of a relief in several vertical planes (Pls. 22, 24). The back of the main figure, when the figure is carved in the round, is only sketched and assimilated to the slab of the stele.

The relation of the plastic conception and its actual presentation as mūrti is paradoxical. The inner quality of Indian sculptural form is in the round, in the interpenetration and transitions from globular and pear shapes to conical and cylindrical parts of undulating contours. This three-dimensional quality, however, in the cult image is compacted as stele, a compromise form between sculpture in the round and in relief.

In the rite of approach, which leads straight towards the innermost presence in the temple where it has its end and fulfillment, the image is seen within its frame, the doorway, as one picture composed of architectural space and sculpture, linked by glowing lights and engulfing darkness. All these elements form one composition of which the image is the centre. In certain images, like that of the Sun god (Pl. 24), the carved slab is conceived as a chariot on which the image drives forth from transcendental reality into manifestation, from invisible realms into the field of vision. Within the ensconcing darkness of the sanctuary (garbha-gṛha, the "womb-chamber"), the image or symbol manifests out of a plenum as its illuminated kernel and centre.

This setting of the image is the form given to the vision itself as it takes place in the mind of the imager. According to the canonical text of a trance-formula of visualisation (sādhana; dhyāna),[22] the mind draws the deity to itself as though from a great distance where the archetypes are in heaven—that is immediately from the inner space of the heart where the realisation dwells deeply hidden in its cave.[23] There the image

[22] B. Bhattacharya, *The Buddhist Indian Iconography* (1924), pp. 169 f. Cf. A. K. Coomaraswamy, *The Transformation of Nature in Art* (Dover Publications, 1956), p. 6.

[23] Cf. *Kaṭha Upaniṣad,* 1.2.12.

is beheld and realised inwardly. The mental-visual image gets into shape in the heart. There the intuition in its lightning speed is hewn out[24] as if by a carpenter's adze. The vision in the heart acquires its form and definition as if by an act of sculpture; the actual form of the vision, the concrete image, appears in the dark space of the shrine, which is a hypostasis of the dark cave of the heart. It is its architectural form. The vision, the mental image, appears to the sculptor in plastic terms. The concrete image, then, is given the form and setting as he lived it in his own body in its inmost recess. The creative process itself has become objectified and projected into form. The image arises in the inner field of vision. Its place, according to Indian notion, is the heart where man faces God and creates His image. This secret space itself, together with the inner vision in its depth, are projected into the concrete form in which the image (mūrti) appears in the innermost sanctuary of the temple.

In this position, the image functions as the support of the devotee's contemplation and helps him to come closest to the divinity which is ritually installed in the image and embodied by its form. The order of the form is regulated by a canon of proportions and codified postures, gestures, and attributes. These define the nature of the particular divinity. To the devotee, each part of the image has meaning. The contents of the image definable by name and number are laid out before him not only as a cognisance, but also as proportionate parts of the total plastic conception, in the shape of the limbs of the image and its facial features.[25] By the aid of the parts of the image, the devotee builds up the divine presence before his eye, limb by limb from the feet upwards to the chest, head, and crown, and to the arms with their attributes. He dwells on each part[26] where the flux of the modelling is accentuated by the ornaments and draperies clinging to the smooth, rounded planes of the body. The eye's pilgrimage, having halted at the many stations full of meaning, yields the beatific vision of the whole. The indivisible form of the image and its indwelling power are now consciously seen by the devotee. Such seeing with the eye of knowledge requires and brings detachment from everything whatever but the presence of the image. Towards it the devotee has the most intense attachment, for he ritually touches with his gaze the part of the image on which he concentrates, and he touches with his hands his own body at those same places, effecting a magic transfer of his living self, whereby he is oned with the deity. Man becomes what he worships.[27]

The vision of the deity being set forth in its image, the devotee, by magic transfer, identifies himself throughout his living body with the image, so that the vision

[24] *Ṛig Veda,* 10.71.8, "hṛdā taṣṭeṣu manaso javeṣu."

[25] Cf. the chart of canons of proportionate measurement as given in Stella Kramrisch, *Viṣṇudharmottara* (Calcutta, 1928), Introduction, pp. 23–28.

[26] Mahānirvāṇa Tantra, 13.289–291; 13.293–297.

[27] The *Bhagavadgītā* (9.25) says: "Votaries of the gods go to the gods; votaries of the Fathers go to the Fathers; votaries of goblins go to the goblins. . . ."

arises in him. He is then no longer in need of the image. In this respect, the image serves as a magic place of transformation. It is entered at will by rites of purification, and it is left by rites of leave-taking. The image—the work of art—ceases to exist for the devotee unless it is the sole object of his concentration and self-identification. Correspondingly, images made of clay for domestic, seasonal worship are immersed after use in the water of a river or pond nearby, where they soon disintegrate into the mud of which they were made. Year after year, new images must be made for definite festivals for every household. Again and again divinity is invoked and appears to the craftsman for the short meeting while he makes the image, and divinity is established in the consecrated image for worship.

The underlying conviction in this incessant new making and then destroying of the image is that the vision is aeviternal in heaven and indefatigable in its return to earth. Faith in the incessant renewal of creativeness decrees that the concrete image must be looked upon only with the look of knowledge, under conditions when nothing else is seen but the image, when the devotee transfers and thereby transmits his being into that of the image. This is the effect of the image on the beholder and the only way in which it can be seen and known. Ever anew, the vision is seen and made concrete, and, ever again, its concrete image is destroyed so that it can be formed afresh and draw to itself the resources of the moment. Then the deity is beheld in the ever changing moods in which the living moment moulds the eternal image.

Cult images constitute only a small part of the temple sculptures. A large and fully evolved temple may carry nearly a thousand sculptures on its walls. It has but one central cult image in the innermost sanctuary. This image embodies the divinity to whom the temple is consecrated. It is itself but one of the aspects in which God is conceived and made manifest. "Whatsoever form any devotee seeks to worship with faith, that very form I ordain to be for each . . ." are the words of Lord Kṛiṣṇa in the *Bhagavadgītā* (7.21). That very form of each manifestation inhabits the image in the innermost sanctuary and is made visible on the outside of the temple in its further aspects in the light of day.

The majority of Hindu temples are dedicated to Śiva and Viṣṇu. Śiva is the principle and the manifestation of divinity from which all originates and in which all is resolved. He brings this world into existence and takes it back into himself. Viṣṇu is the principle and manifestation which pervade and safeguard existence. The icon, or symbol, of these great gods is in the innermost sanctuary ensconced in the masonry of the temple and faces its entrance. The other three sides of the temple carry in the middle and main buttress of their outer wall the image of one of the main, or most closely related, aspects of the deity enshrined in the temple. These are, in the case of Viṣṇu, his avatars, of which only three are carved, each facing in one of the cardinal directions. An avatar is that symbolic form which the Lord who maintains life assumes in order to protect it at those cosmic crises when life is bent on its own destruction and evil prevails. It is then that Lord Viṣṇu descends (avatarati) from his state of glory. Assuming that form which is adequate to the particular crisis, he rescues creation, as Fish-avatar (Pl. 48) or as Boar-avatar, or as Rāma, the King (p. 100), or as Lord Kṛiṣṇa, or as the Buddha.

In a Śiva temple, the three main positions facing the orients are held not by the "descents" of the god, but by several of his aspects or by extensions of his power as it works through the goddess, his wife, Pārvatī, and his sons, elephant-headed Gaṇeśa, the Lord of hosts, and Kārttikeya, whom the Pleiades nursed (Pl. 9).

These divinities facing the main directions are "collateral gods" of the Presence in the icon or symbol in the womb-chamber. Images of these Pārśvadevatās, like those of the main image, are in the shape of a stele; and this, as a rule, is placed in a niche of the central buttress of the wall. These images, so closely associated with the central icon, follow the norm that applies to it.

The norm is the consolidated tradition which guarantees the identity of vision and image as far as it can be laid down in named shape and number. The named shape includes the description of face and limbs of the image, its youth, beauty, expression and gestures, raiments, adornments, and objects associated with the deity. All these data are laid down in formulae called dhyāna, or mental representation of the attributes of divinity. Their collection would yield a complete corpus and history of Indian iconography. The dhyāna belongs to the technique of evoking the image at will. It is a trance-formula for induced vision. The perfection, character, and movement of face and body of the image are controlled by proportion. The science of proportionate measurement (tālamāna) gives the norms for each type of image, male or female, in canons which are adjusted to the hierarchy of the invisible world in its extent from gods to demons, sprites and gnomes.

The proportions of the images conform with those of the temple. The height of the Liṅga or the image in the "womb-chamber," the innermost sanctuary or cavity in the temple-piles, is, according to several schools of architecture, the module of the building.[28]

[28] *The Hindu Temple,* chart on p. 232A. The width of the outside of the wall of the sanctuary was thrice the height of the image or Liṅga. The proportions in plan and elevation are multiples and submultiples of the width of the wall.

Rājarāṇī Temple, Part of Wall and Superstructure. S. Bhuvaneshvar, Orissa. *Photograph Eliot Elisofon*

Kandariyā Temple, Part of Wall and Superstructure. Khajurāho, Madhya Pradesh.

5

Sculpture, the Form of Architecture

SCULPTURE IN INDIA is a comprehensive form. Its total monument is the entire temple. Its mass is organised in salient shapes which carry and delimit or alternate with statues and reliefs. The profiles of the architectural mouldings are symmetrical and consonant with the modelling of the figures. Together they form the closely knit pattern of the wall laid out three dimensionally, in the changing play of light and shade. The structural problems are solved with sculptural effect foremost in mind. The outside of the temple, with its towering superstructure, has the effect of an architectural solid, while the interior enshrines, under the pile of the superstructure closed off from view by a ceiling, the small "womb-chamber" (garbha-gṛha). While most of the stone temples are structural, others are cut out of solid rock. The paradox of rock-cut temples, such as those of Ellora or Kalugumalai, in the likeness of structural shrines, becomes plausible because the underlying conception, even of the structural temples, is sculptural and not architectural. The rock-cut temple, even technically, is a work of sculpture. Whether cut out of the rock or set up in space, the form of the monument is sculptural. Sculpture is the dominant mode of Indian form from the beginning of Indian art history. Painting, too, through the first millennium, is illusionistically three-dimensional, modelling, as sculpture does, its shapes, albeit by painterly means, by line, colour, and shading, so that the figures stand out from their ground in interlacing rhythms of their phantasmagoric presence.

The plan of the fully evolved temple is conceived from its centre and has the square as its primal form. The square of the womb-chamber is enclosed by four walls whose thickness on the outside is augmented by broad facets or buttresses, the major projection being in the middle of each face. This results in a cruciform or star-shaped ground plan of the outer side of the bulwark of walls. While the building faces the four directions, it has no façade. In certain regional schools, like that of Orissa, the entrance is the only opening of the temple proper, which has no windows.

The temple proper (prāsāda or vimāna) is the monument which encloses and towers over the womb-chamber. It is complete in itself, though it may have a porch or one or more halls in front of the entrance. But, all these accessory parts or separate buildings lie in one line which is the main axis of the entire temple compound. The walls of the accessory buildings show variations of the theme of the walls of the temple proper.

The walls of the temple arise from a plinth. Above, they are shaded by a cornice. It is there that their vertical extent terminates, and the superstructure is raised within curvilinear planes in nearly all the temples excepting those of South India, where the superstructure has the shape of a pyramid. The Museum collection consists of images and of stone sculptures which once were part of temple walls. There is also in the Museum an entire interior of a South Indian temple hall (ardha-maṇḍapa) (Pl. 55).[29]

The figure sculptures are displayed on the buttressed exterior of the vertical walls of the majority of Indian temples—they are classified as Nāgara—between the mouldings of the base and those of the cornice. Below, in the base, in the horizontal recesses of its mouldings, in panels or friezes, is the life in this temporal world, with its music and dance (Pl. 37), with its warriors (Pl. 39), hunters, lovers, with scenes of religious discourse (Pl. 27), or of masons at work. The frieze above, however, where it occurs as part of the cornice of the walls, shows the deeds of the gods (Osia) and the inexhaustible array of the celestial host. These carvings are on a small scale. They are shaded over by mouldings; their effect is subordinated to that of the vertical themes on the staggered walls of the buttresses. (Text illustrations, pp. 42A, B.) Their vertical projections start from the ground. They belong to both base and wall. These they bind into one unit whose lower part forms the projected socle of the vertical walls of the buttress. The further the main buttress is projected in the middle of the wall, the deeper is the adjacent vertical recess of the wall from which the next buttress springs forth to a lesser distance than the main buttress.[30] On the fully evolved temples, moreover, from the ninth and tenth centuries onward, each buttress has its own offsets in front and also on the sides. Its corners are recessed. Frequently, this indentation is repeated so that the front facet of the buttress is removed by two steps from the main body of that buttress. Its staggered vertical planes form a pier, detached from the next pier by a vertical and deeply shaded chase of similarly stepped planes. This theme of indentation is extended also to the horizontal mouldings of the wall (vedikā). In temples which have in addition to a socle, even a subsocle, these gradations in parallel, vertical planes are further extended to both these lowermost horizontally piled-up parts, with their progressively projected mouldings, until in their maximum extension they rest on the ground.

The mouldings of cyma, torus, fillet shape, or "knife-edged," sparkling with variegated, vertical facets like crystals of a chandelier, are bound into the ascending order of the piers by the striations, at rhythmical intervals of deep recesses and cavettos hold-

[29] W. Norman Brown, *A Pillared Hall From a Temple at Madura,* (Philadelphia, 1940). *Handbook of the Far Eastern Wing,* Philadelphia Museum of Art (1958), p. 25.

[30] The description given here and in the following pages is generally in order to evoke the original setting of the sculptures in the collection of the Museum.

ing shade in different densities. This abstract sculpture composed of architectural parts is, furthermore, accentuated by diminutive carvings of architectural motifs and minute figures which enhance the mouldings.

Miniature sculpture is a particularly Indian branch of sculpture. Unlike miniature painting, it is not a reduced aspect of the art with a consequently circumscribed impact. The actual dimensions of an Indian sculpture do not determine its form, which is conceived on the same scale of proportions, irrespective of the unit of measurement. The quality of Indian sculpture is monumental in any size.

The bulwark of the temple walls offers its sculptures in horizontal, as well as in vertical, rhythmic sequences on the offsets, in the depth of the chases, and also on the connecting wall surfaces at right angles to offsets and chases. (Text illustrations, pp. 42A, B.) On each of these walls, the large figures represent the furthermost progression of that wall in the shape of sculptural form alive with modelling and specific meaning (Pls. 26, 38, 32). They are underscored by the horizontal sequence of the small relief panels (Pls. 27, 37) between the mouldings extended from pier to pier and across the darkness of the vertical chases which separate the buttresses. The mouldings run along with the articulation of the monument, in and out of the recesses into which their profiles project, and where they almost seem to meet in space.

In this sculptured orchestration of the monument, each single pier is an offshoot of its total mass and a diminutive replica of its form. Proceeding upward beyond the height of the vertical wall, each of its piers is extended on the superstructure (Śikhara), or the piers carry superstructures of their own, each a miniature replica of the central towering shape.

The virtual pivot of this monumental mass, with its theme of projected offsets, is in the interior of the womb-chamber. It rises where the Liṅga or the icon stands. From this central axis, the monument is planned with the images on its walls. These are, it has been shown, figured projections of the central indwelling power (p. 39). They step forth, together with the walls. The Pārśvadevatās (Pls. 9, 30), the collateral gods, facing the orients, on the central, furthermost projected buttress, are housed in niches, whose sheltered recess adumbrates the interior of the womb-chamber. The impact of the total bulwark is carried forward step by step and meets the devotee, while he walks around the temple. Whereas, the Pārśvadevatās are immersed in the shadows of their niches, the carvings on the other piers are proffered into open spaces. They are on view, not only from the front as are the icons, but also can be seen in almost as many profiles as sculpture in the round (Pls. 17, 45). Yet they are attached to the pier from which they project. They are carved from the same stone and in a particular way. While they are, for the most part, carved in the round, if their head is shown in profile or their body turned towards the wall, the portion of the figure which is closest to the wall is lengthened towards the wall. This protraction extends over a depth greater than that which the figure would occupy were it carved in the round. By this distortion, the figure gradually emerges from the plane of the ground to the high relief of the front view. It appears as if carved in the round; whereas, a side view shows the "fore-lengthening" of the respective part, as if the figure would disengage itself gradually from the stone out of which it is carved, engendering in this process a sketchlike prefiguration of its fully manifest shape.

The sculptures of the temple wall representing the lesser hierarchies surpass the icons by the spontaneity of their conception. They are proffered from the body of the monument together with the stepped procession of the buttress. (Text illustrations, pp. 42A, B.) Each image however is the final exposition of the indwelling energy and meaning of the monument at that particular part, an ever renewed charge on the sensibility and receptiveness of the devotee. Their effect and effectiveness are conveyed not by the figure or configuration by itself, but by the total impact of the monument. The graded, projected planes sustain and articulate the projection of the figures towards the devotee from a depth which is indicated by the chases between the piers. The single sculptures carry with them a monumental movement of the mass. They are charged with a propelling energy which goes into their form. The impact of the sculptures of the temple wall transcends that of any sculpture independently conceived, for they are designed as part of the total image, the temple. They are imbued with the power of this entire gigantically intricate conception. It is not that they belong to any particular architectural theme as do caryatids or gothic pillar figures, the one incorporating the function of support, which the other denies expressing transcendence of earthly weight. Indian temple sculptures have no structural function in the monument. They are carried by its theme and propelled from its bulk. In the shape of specified figures, they are exposed centrifugally from the total mass of the bulwark.

The temple itself is house and body of God. It is articulate in its proportions. These bind together all the parts of the monument, whether these are in the likeness of images based on the figure of man or whether they represent architectural themes. For the latter, too, as they are employed on the temple walls, are embodiments of content. They are also replicas of more ancient and originally structural shapes. They are divested of any structural function which they had in their original use, just as the human figure is divested of its functions when represented in sculpture. Window motives (gavākṣa, "ray-eye"), for example, are carved in relief without any opening to admit light. They are employed singly, framing the heads of celestials or lion shapes or the blank ground. They are combined and form courses (gavākṣmālā), or they fill large surfaces with their diminutive, contiguous, indefinitely repeated curvilinear eyelets. Their contours are reminiscent of the curves of their original bamboo frame. As symbolic enhancement of the surface which they cover, they are suggestive of the innumerable eyes by which the divine presence enshrined in the monument looks out into all the planes of existence on all of its sides. Such enrichments on the temple walls, whose original elements fulfilled architectural functions, are used conjointly with the images in the shape of man and animal. Both the "architectural" and the figured enrichments function as symbols. By their order and disposition over all the planes of the monument, they give exposition to its meaning which arises from the ground plan of the temple.

In the contemplative, peripatetic movement of the devotee, the piers and angles, planes and profiles offer a continuous panorama, a "moving picture," whose every moment has form and meaning. When the devotee halts in his walk, his eye is led upward by the piers. They have their continuation on the generally curved planes of the superstructure to which they cling, carrying in these high levels almost exclusively "abstract," non-figured symbolical patterns towards the high point of the finial (pp. 42A, B).

Seeing the temple, while approaching and walking around it, is an exercise in cognising the order of existence. The disposition of the figure sculptures and the sequences of monumental themes are the ladders on which the eye climbs the cosmic mountain. The temple-massive rises in its likeness. It is surmounted, above the bulk of its shape, by the finial pointing into the empyrean beyond form.

The single sculptures in the Museum, which are fragments from temple walls (Pls. 35, 41, 45), must be imagined in this their context. In their modelled volumes each one of them brings home the impact of the temple wall of which it was part.

On the vertical walls, as pointed out already, the Pārśvadevatās (Pls. 9, 30) face the orients from their niches in the middle buttress of each wall. They face the three directions while the main direction—the East, as a rule—is faced by the icon (Pls. 22, 24) or Liṅga (Pl. 49) in the womb-chamber, through the entrance or across the halls in front of it, their doorways lying in one and the same axis. The other piers are occupied by the images of the guardians of the eight regions (Pl. 32). They protect the orients and the intermediate directions. On the piers between those of the Pārśvadevatās and the guardians of the regions are displayed the "tree-woman" (Pl. 38), the Surasundarīs and Apsarasas, and ancillary (parivāra) gods (Pl. 45); while in the recesses and elsewhere dwell couples in embrace (mithuna [Pl. 14]), or Chimaeras (śārdūla [Pl. 34]).

6

Types of Temple Sculpture

WITHIN THE GENERAL scheme sketched above, the carvings and the walls of the Nāgara temple vary in their relation in the regional schools. Each school has its own logic whose working can be followed, as in Orissa, through the centuries. Other and equally distinct regional schools of the Nāgara form of monumental sculpture are, however, preserved only in one or the other of their phases.

The majority of single sculptures in the Museum were part of Nāgara temples, some of whose main types are represented by the eastern Indian school of Orissa and by the Mid-Indian school of which the temples of Khajurāho are the most important group (Pls. 6–18, 29–37).

The term regional school is taken from western usage, where the art of a country is referred to as the French school, or Italian school, or English school. The style, whether Gothic, Renaissance, or Baroque, extends over all these countries. The Indian regional schools belong to areas as large or larger than some countries of Europe, each having its own climate, physically and on all the other levels of experience. The masters who created the form of each region are generally anonymous. Even where an inscribed name (pp. 92, 93) or a portrait (Pl. 56B) is known to us, its incidental occurrence on a monument is not sufficient to connect the manner and quality of a particular work with the signed name or the portrait. The monuments are the collective work not only of one master and his pupils, but of several masters and their workshops. Even so, the creative genius, as seen in the continuous work of a region, is distinct. The ancient Indians spoke of the genius loci as Yakṣa. Ruling dynasties, by conquests and alliances, extended the limits, as well as the range, of the genius loci. Master craftsmen would be sent to conquered land and would, in new countries, contribute their traditions to those practised on the spot, adding a new mode to an already extant form.

The genius loci can be seen, particularly in Orissa, in the flexibility of its impress in styles of successive periods. They unfold with the logic of a living organism in contact with others and enriched by them. The wall sculptures of the earliest Orissan temples, but for the images of the Pārśvadevatās and their collateral images on adjacent buttresses, are carved in a relatively low relief (Pls. 6, 7). The stone walls appear as if encrusted with carvings. They seem to give to the stone of the walls a new texture, speckled with light and shade and streaked and reticulated, in regular intervals, with black lines of shadow. These are provided by the vertical offsets and the recesses between the mouldings of the monument.

Sculpture as an integument of the surface of the monument, giving to the texture of the stone a richer substantiality, is a special quality of the early Orissan temples (eighth century). Other temples of this phase in northern India are not as enmeshed in their sequences of carved units. These are more distinctly separated or widely spaced (Telika Mandir, Gwalior; temples in Nachna-Kuthara or Osia, for example). Two reliefs (Pls. 6, 7) from temples now decayed in Bhuvaneshvar, Orissa, were once part of surfaces textured with carvings as are the walls of the temple of Paraśurāmeśvara in Bhuvaneshvar.

In the next phase of monumental sculpture in Orissa, of which the Vaitāl Deul in Bhuvaneshvar[31] and the Śiśireśvara too are representative, an increased height of the relief is accommodated within frames which are doubly and triply stepped. Only the major images of the Paraśurāmeśvara temple were similarly framed. In this phase, the broad, but also much fuller, volume of the figures, though encased within the deep frame, appears pressed outward from its container. At times, an arm, a crown, a weapon, or part of a drapery overlaps one of the interior frames of the panel of the offset. Corresponding to the stepped recesses of the panels let into the front of the offsets, the sides of these pilasters, too, are similarly stepped. Their narrow vertical planes recede in graded shade into the darkness of the vertical chase between them and the next offset with its similarly stepped facets. The light is conducted gradually towards the depth of the chases in half-tones between and around the images. In this harmonious setting, the image of "Durgā Killing the Buffalo Titan" (Pl. 8) would have occupied the niche of a central buttress of a temple somewhat earlier than the Vaitāl Deul.

Notwithstanding their amplitude and the assurance of their disposition, the figure sculptures are still, as they were on the Paraśurāmeśvar temple, within the wall surface. Within their deep frames, they are set as if in showcases. In this relief style, the opulently conceived figures are modelled nearly, and in parts fully, in the round. Their flexed, sturdy bodies and limbs are laid out between the ground of the relief and its framing surface. They now no longer are mere entities in a reticulated, textured form in which they have position, but no space of their own. The figures dwell in closely set receptacles, each figure or group filling the allotted space in three dimensions, as much by their bold volumes as by the directions of their movements. They are confined within the wall in a strict, but also extreme, fulfillment of this discipline of relief sculpture. But whether the reliefs appear as part of the textured surface of the building or as

[31] H. Zimmer, *The Art of Asian India,* Pl. 326. P. Rambach and V. de Golish, *The Golden Age of Indian Art,* Pls. 61, 63–65. Stylistically, the temple can be assigned to the late eighth century. It is also known as Temple of Kapālinī Devī.

images encased in the thickness of the wall, they are bounded and contained within the monumental planes.

In the following centuries, the figures on the piers were to become the foremost exponents of the walls in their progressive projection into space, into the light of day, and into the graded shade in the deepening chases and recesses. Their chiaroscuro now furrows with space volumes the mass of the temple bulwark but does not dissolve its continuity of ascent nor its outward impact. With increasing articulateness in depth, the carvings of the foremost plane on the facetted projections of walls and superstructure connect the many striations that lie further back in depth. In the strong light of the Indian sun, the carvings on the highest plane of the offsets in the superstructure (śikhara) appear like a veil tautly stretched over the mouldings and recesses ensconced behind their tracery in airy layers of carved space.

In the early phase, the reliefs seemed encrusted on the surface of the stone, giving it a texture of meaningful patterns on the piers and their strata. In the maturity of the school, the compact walls of the Orissan monuments open up in graded chases and recesses. On the vertical temple walls, the large images are set off against intricately detailed planes further back in space. Their surfaces are covered with diminutive modelled or obliquely cut patterns whose texture is vibrant in contrasts and transitions of light and dark. Against these low-relief, surface patterns on the several receding facets of their buttresses the larger images stand out in a counterpoint of their fully modelled shapes set forth into space and light, and the bulwark of the walls behind them. (Text illustration, p. 42A.) The volume of the bulwark is closely interknit. The piers with their facets, traversed below and above the images by multiform mouldings, are the meshes in which all degrees of shade are caught in chases and recesses. The volume of the monument is now composed of stone and space bounded and controlled by the indented plan of the monument.

The images are upheld, each on a socle of its own (temples of Mukteśvara and Rājarāṇī) proportionate with the height of the figure. In an ultimate fulfillment of their centrifugal role, they are bodied forth completely in the round, detached from the wall, on the eaves of the temple of Koṇārak (mid-thirteenth century).[32]

Set forth from the wall in this highest degree of corporeal form, the figures are an ultimate fulfillment of the temple monument conceived as sculpture. In their form and meaning, they embody its inherent power and manifest its energies.

In the earlier phases, all the carvings, whether of figures, architecture, symbols, or scrolls, had been integrated in the wall. In the maturity of the school of Orissa, the major images project beyond the foremost planes of their piers. These planes throughout their length are now filled with carpetlike panels of scrolls whose patterns are dominated by the symbol of the wave. The scrolls are curly, conglomerated, lambent shapes carved

[32] *The Art of Indian Asia,* Pls. 362, 363.

aslant and modelled. The wave is either the principle of organisation in currents and eddies or it is carved as a stalk sending out tendrils and leaves, engulfing the figures of animals, sprites, gnomes, and nameless configurations of the sculptor's imagination (Pl. 15). Each of these compositions is a self-contained pattern of creative agitation.

The motif of the obliquely cut scroll has a long history. It is known in stone carvings of Mathurā in Uttar Pradesh, in the fifth century A.D., and occurs subsequently in the Deccan (Paṭṭadakal, eighth century) and in the extreme South of India (Kalugumalai, ca. ninth century). It found its richest soil in Orissa, particularly in the later phases of this school, where its devices effect a final transmutation of the grain of the stone into the plastic texture of the temple wall.[33]

The transmutation of the grain of the stone surface into a carved texture full of meaning comes about both spontaneously and methodically, for it is vested in the knowledge which the Indian sculptor has of the building stones. This knowledge obviously implies the experience of their surface by touch and their resistance to his tools, but this practical knowledge is accompanied by a deeper understanding of the building stones of the temple. In the rite of building the temple, the building stones are known and invoked as goddesses and are addressed by their names and attributes, for they are realised as fraught with power. This power is communicated to them from the divine presence of which the central image or symbol in the inmost sanctuary is the seat.[34]

The "material" itself of his work, the substance which the hands of the sculptor give form to, is a potent medium. Ideologically it carries and creatively it evokes the power which wants to become form in abstract design and iconographic definition. Abstract relief composition, the ryhthmical transformation of the wall panels into vital pattern, is one of the themes of temple sculpture. It has more than one application. Its widest scope is in the wall panels organised by the wave. These panels, although abstract in appearance where they are altogether without figure, are nonetheless expressive of a definite scheme, that of the wave. The pattern of the wave has a definite meaning. The "creeper of wish-fulfillment," the Kalpalatā, rambles through all these panels, exuberant in producing forms shaped by emotion.

Another application of abstract composition is provided by the perforated stone windows of temple halls. The stone slabs which are to form the windows are carved on their outside with figures (Pl. 48) and scenes. These are cut out along part of the outlines of the figures in bold and irregular spaces. Seen from inside the hall in the building which precedes the sanctuary, the window frame is filled with an irregular, though vaguely rhythmical, perforated, abstract design of plain stone links. Like the leading of a stained glass window, they surround bright, colourful fragments, which here are of sunlit air and the scene outside. Although the abstract design of the perforated stone window is

[33] *Ibid.*, Pls. 341–43.

[34] *The Hindu Temple*, p. 112.

only a by-product of the figured relief facing the outside of the building, the effect of this design transforms a dark interior into a magic volume of penumbral space. Perforated stone windows full of figure, image, or symbol do not belong only to the Orissan school. They are also known in Madhya Pradesh (Nachna-Kuthara, ca. eighth century), in the Himālaya (Chambā, ca. eleventh century [Pl. 48]), in the Deccan, and in South India.

Technically, the perforated relief belongs also to the icon itself, where the figure of the main divinity has its slab cut off around its contour, so that its shape stands out more from the surrounding divinities which form its entourage (Pls. 9, 12, 22, 24). The modes of carving the self-contained work of sculpture, the icon, and those of carving the total monument are the same. Sculpture is the form of Indian architecture, the icon being specifically, and the temple totally, the seat of divinity and its concrete form (mūrti).[35]

The paradoxical relation of content and form whereby a whole building is conceived as sculpture makes the monument articulate with sculptures whose shapes are based on symbols. These symbols need not actually be shown, as the instance of the wave proves; or they are given shape in the likeness of architectural motifs—such as the gavākṣa or the miniature temple—or they appear in the shape of man. All these symbolic shapes are subsumed in the monument to one symbolic form.

Another relation of figure and monument is represented by the Mid-Indian school with Khajurāho for its centre. Many of the sculptures in the Museum belong to this area (Pls. 29–37). The school is called Candella school after the dynasty that ruled over the region when the temples in Khajurāho were built. The majority of the temples in Khajurāho date from the second half of the tenth and eleventh centuries.[36]

Theirs is a stern magnificence of architectural and figural elements. There are few wave and scroll enhanced surfaces. The walls proffer their pure planes and sharp angles in forceful contrast to the curved shapes of images and mouldings. (Text illustration, p. 42B.) The chiaroscuro in the recesses adds no mellowness but deepens a drama of concision and voluptuousness in which plastic form is staged in Khajurāho.

Other regional centres of temple sculpture in Mid-India and Rājasthān similarly give effect to the dramatic conflict shown at its height in Khajurāho. Chronologically this conflict coincides with the efflorescence of sculptural form of the Orissa temples. In spite of their distinctness, both these leading schools keep pace in their stylistic maturing. The salience of relief and buttresses, the interpenetration and orchestration of space volumes and masses of light and shade are of the same degree, though different in kind, in these

[35] *Ibid.*, p. 165.

[36] The earliest inscribed sculpture in Khajurāho is dated in 922. If the inscriptions of 954 and 1002 refer to the temples of Lakṣmanji and Viśvanātha respectively, their styles of sculpture would precede that of the Kandariyā and other temples. Re the date of the inscription of the Pārśvanātha (Jīnanātha) temple, see S. K. Mitra, *The Early Rulers of Khajuraho* (Calcutta, 1958), p. 223, and B. L. Dhama, *A Guide to Khajuraho* (Bombay, 1927), p. 23.

two leading schools. (Text illustrations, pp. 42A and B.) In the earlier centuries, the regional schools were relatively closer in their interrelation of monumental and plastic form to that of the Orissan monuments as is shown by temples of about the eighth century in Nachna-Kuthara[37] in Mid-India and in Osia in Rājasthān. The two leading schools are farthest apart at the height of exposition of their specific trends.

At this phase, the tenth and eleventh centuries, the idioms of the regional schools are most particularly their own. Within the Eastern school the masses of Orissan sculptures (Pls. 9–11) cohere with greater breadth and tension than the columnar volumes of Pāla sculpture in Bihār and Bengal (Pls. 21, 22). The latter school shapes its figures and also their details as separate entities. The often meticulous definitions of the shapes of Pāla sculpture seem conceived by the waking consciousness of the sculptor, whereas it is his dream consciousness which seems to flow directly into the greater specific density of Orissan form. Both these schools are more insistent on detailed plastic statements than those of central India.

The central Indian schools are less concerned with detailed modelling. Those situated to the north, of which the Candella school is representative, enliven a gravid volume with sensuous tremors (Pls. 36, 37). Further to the south, the Haihaya school charges its masses with a vehement, three-dimensional impact. With an eruptive urgency, shapes surge into closeness. Towards the west, the sculptures of Mālwā are compacted of staid volumes (Pls. 44, 45).

The various centres in Rājasthān suffuse with delicacy (Pls. 38, 39) or heighten with brisk accents (Pls. 42, 43) a form which they share with the Candella and allied schools to the east. In these schools of Rājasthān and central India, in the later tenth and eleventh centuries, a new form was created within their inherited mould. Its power is greatest in the Candella school and in southern Rājasthān where it presses the convex planes of the figures to an extreme bulge and connects the silhouettes of vaulted chest and jutting buttocks, by a deep hollow of the back. The resulting concave appearance of the body is met by that of the legs curved in the opposite direction, in a frenzy of three-dimensional torsion and linear clarity. To this vital and paradoxical form the faces of the images respond with angular profiles and equivocal expressions (Pls. 31, 33).

[37] Stella Kramrisch, *The Art of India,* Pls. 107, 115, 116.

7

Schools of Sculpture Represented in the Museum

Mathurā and Gandhāra

IN THE EARLY centuries of our era two schools of art in the north of the subcontinent were momentous in the history of Buddhist art and Indian iconography. The one had its centre in Mathurā, the "city of the gods" on the river Yamunā. The other extended over the northwestern frontier in the mountain regions of Gandhāra in Pakistan, and Afghanistan, and is known as the Gandhāra school. Both the schools flourished under the same foreign dynasty, the Kuṣāṇas. Mathurā met an Indian demand for images with the resources of an indigenous school. Gandhāra satisfied a frontier population with the work of local talent in touch with Indian tradition and exposed to the impression made by the art of the Western world.

In the first centuries of the school the work of Gandhāra was eclectic and ecclesiastic. From the third century to its end (sculptures of Fondukistan,[38] seventh century) the work of the school of Gandhāra came alive, integrated Western classical ideals and conventions with a compassionate Buddhist outlook (Pl. 5), and kept pace with contemporary Indian art. Mathurā under the Kuṣāṇas expanded the traditions of its school. In a manner of their own they were imbued with a Mahāyāna outlook. Robust and self-assured, Kuṣāṇa images and figures proclaim the joy of life (Pls. 2B, 3). If, according to the Mahāyāna doctrine, any existent thing in itself is nothing and has no separate inward reality, all existent things in this respect are equal. The devaluation of reality levels existence and brings to the fore the sensual factors which early Buddhism had disciplined. A Yakṣī in early Buddhist art is as earnest and selfless in her presence as the worshipper on a railing pillar from Bhuvaneshvar (Pl. 1). A Yakṣī, carved in Mathurā of the Kuṣāṇa school (Pl. 3), is buxom and confident in her worship. The naive, at times even coarse, sensuality of the Yakṣī figures of the Mathurā school has its legitimate place on a sacred

[38] B. Rowland, *The Art and Architecture of India,* Pl. 61.

monument. It is a genuine expression, consistent in its form, and consistent with the knowledge that such a sculpture has as much reality as "the daughter of a barren virgin carved in stone."

The plasticity of Indian sculpture takes to itself, in the Mathurā school, the palpitations of the flesh of the thighs (Pl. 3) or the cheeks (Pl. 2B) of its figures in one of the recurrent situations when the Indian sculptor dwells on the physical body, the outer envelope, full of power and three-dimensional impact (Pl. 4).

The later schools of Indian sculpture belong to the age of the monumental stone temples. The relation of figure and monument in some of the major schools has already been outlined. Although the collection of the Museum is not large, it is representative of some of the currents and achievements of Indian sculpture from the eighth to the seventeenth centuries and beyond it.

The Eastern School

ORISSA The schools of sculpture, though they do not fully coincide in their geographical extent with particular linguistic areas, are at home in areas where the ethnic blend resulted in a distinct physiognomical type of the majority of the people characteristic of the region. The form of the work of a school, however, is not affected by the scene in which it is at home. In the Orissa school, for example, where successive styles of sculpture can be followed from about the eighth to the thirteenth century and later, it would be difficult to find distinctive traits in the work of the coastal region as against the hilly hinterland. Differences there are as within any unified output, even within the work of one master. In Orissa, the differences are subsumed to the form of sculpture created by the Uriya-speaking people.[39] Where their country borders on Bengal, a blend of both the Orissa and the Bengal style is seen in the sculptures of Māyurbhañj.[40] The art of this small territory, though it shows its midway position between the schools of Bengal and Orissa, has a self-consistent form equal in quality to those of the greater regions. Taken together, these three regional schools, from about the eighth century, are generally considered to form one school, that of Eastern India. The school extends over Bihār in the west. The school of Bengal and Bihār under the rule of the Pāla and Sena dynasties, from ca. 800 to 1200, is one.

Eastern Indian sculpture is well represented in the collection of the Museum. The images from Bengal and Bihār can no longer be visualised in their original setting,

[39] The school extended to the South into Ganjam where the Someśvara temple at Mukhalinga is one of the most accomplished creations of this school. Cf. Stella Kramrisch "Kaliṅga temples," *Journal of the Indian Society of Oriental Art,* II (1934), Pl. XVIII.3.

[40] R. P. Chanda, *The Bhañja Dynasty of Māyurbhañj* (Māyurbhañj, 1929), Pls. 1–24.

because most of the brick temples—and all wooden shrines—of which they formed part have perished. The Orissan sculptures in the Museum are images and sculptures of the temple walls. The context of sculptures like these in the total monument has been described. In the early phase the sculptures of Orissa are related to the art of the Northern Deccan,[41] whereas in the later phases this school is more closely related to the art of Bihār and Bengal. Throughout the five centuries of Orissan temple sculpture, however, this school has its distinct qualities irrespective of the preponderance of Deccan form elements in the eighth century. It is by these specifically Orissan qualities of form that this school was to become one of the two leading branches of Eastern Indian sculpture.

The history of sculpture in Orissa can be traced back to the middle of the third century B.C. when the Maurya Emperor Aśoka had his edict engraved at Dhauli near Bhuvaneshvar on the vertical surface of a rock. Out of the midst an elephant emerges, its front half carved in the round, the back of its body hidden in the rock. The traditions of Indian sculpture are seen here in their full application, not only in the plastic modelling of the head of the animal, but also in the context of its figure with the rock in whose mass it remains half hidden while emerging into shape. While the form is Indian, it is not possible here, nor in another carving from Bhuvaneshvar (Pl. 1) two centuries later, to say in what respect these sculptures are distinctly Orissan.[42]

More than a millennium after Aśoka, the earliest temples now known had their walls carved with low reliefs in the cast particular to the Orissan school.[43] In breadth and organisation of the plastic mass, the reliefs are related to the Deccan. The Nāga amidst lotuses (Pl. 6) belongs to this phase (ca. eighth century). The cursive scribble to which the rendering of well-known architectural, symbolical motives is reduced on the left of the panel and the crude, though fluid, generalisation of the lotus plant and the Nāga figure rely on earlier versions of these themes. These earlier versions are known in the rock-cut temples of the Western Deccan, in Kanheri of the sixth century and in Ellora.[44] The Nāga's body emerges in a forceful diagonal movement from the waters—which are not represented—at the bottom of the relief. The tilt of the Nāga's body is balanced by the angle of his head and halolike serpent hood. The bent and raised arm cutting across

[41] The art of the Northern Deccan extends its influence from the Western Ghats through the centre of India to the eastern coast. The sculptures of the temples in Rajim (Raipur) fall into this zone of influence, whereas the sculptures from Sirpur of the same region (Mahākosala) are nearer to the work of the northern Indian schools of the post-Gupta age.

[42] The Dhauli elephant (cf. L. Bachhofer, *Early Indian Sculptures,* Pl. I) contrasts with the pseudo-Achaemenian animal sculptures of the Mauryan age. Few examples only of early sculpture in Orissa are known apart from the rock sculptures of Udayagiri and Khaṇḍagiri.

[43] K. C. Panigrahi, "New Light on the Early History of Bhuvaneśhvara," *Journal of the Asiatic Society,* Letters, CVII (1951), 95–115. T. N. Ramachandran, "The Identification of Two Interesting Sculptures From Orissa," *Journal of Oriental Research,* XIX, Pl. 1.

[44] A. K. Coomaraswamy, *Elements of Buddhist Iconography* (1935), Pl. VII. *The Art of Indian Asia,* Pl. 83.

the body so as to join hands in the gesture of adoration completes the countermovement of head and halo. The slow, creeping curves of the lotus vegetation fill the rest of the panel. They amplify and broaden the upward gesture of the Nāga, around whose figure their buds and leaves close and hold in suspense the impetus of his movement. All this is shown in low relief, in sagging shapes. Like flattened tires, they lie on the ground of the relief. The suspended and somewhat blunted vehemence which is in the composition of the relief corresponds to the facial expression of the heavy-featured Nāga with his sated and contemplative smile. The modelling of his three-quarter profile shows the sculptural maturity which is characteristic of the whole composition, despite its obtuse shapes. The craftsman who carved this small sculpture was no doubt familiar with greater sculptures than his own humble contribution. How many Buddha images, such as those of Ajanta, must have been carved so that the abstractions of their faces could be modified when carried on the shoulders of the lesser hierarchy?

Another small relief (Pl. 7) from a temple of the same age is of monumental quality, although in actual size it belongs to the class of miniature reliefs which have their place on the temple walls next to the larger images of the greater gods. Size, however, is of iconographic and not of artistic moment. The sketchy generalisation of the small body of the female figure, with the globular breasts and broad hips of potential motherhood separated by the thin middle, supports the wide and weighty arc of the arms that spans the width of the panel. The over-large head of the woman rests on it. The profile of the lowered face is modelled in one plane. The forehead and nose are carved with summary sureness, shading within their right angle the unforeshortened eye whose heavy lid holds in covering darkness the pathos of the figure. The lips are shown relaxed. The figure within the raised rim of the stone panel is steeped in the dream of herself.

A mature, three-dimensional sculpture of a preceding phase lends its formulations to the low relief of the two small fragments (Pls. 6, 7). In this, its early phase, Orissan temple sculpture is closer to that of the Deccan than to that of Bihār and owes but little to the last phase of Gupta art practised in the workshops of Sārnāth near Vārāṇasī.[45] The sculpture of Orissa, of ca. the eighth century, in its own specific form is linked with the traditions of sculpture in the Deccan and with those monuments situated between the great sites of cave sculpture in the Western Ghats and the eastern coast, that is with the temple sculptures of Rajim (Raipur).[46]

These Orissan temple sculptures confine to the plane the looming masses of Deccani sculpture. Abstracts and abbreviations of the shapes of Deccani sculpture are spread

[45] Sculptures from northern Orissa (Nalti Giri; Sir Leigh Ashton, *The Art of India and Pakistan* [London, 1949], Fig. 243; R. P. Chanda, "Exploration in Orissa," *Archaeological Survey of India,* Memoir No. 44, Pls. II–VI) of the eighth century show the character of Orissan sculpture based on an intermingling of northeastern (Sārnāth-Vārāṇasī) and Northern-Deccan or central Indian schools.

[46] *The Art of India,* Pl. 106.

out in the surface, distended in their contour, or reduced to a mere scheme, yet the largeness of their original conception is maintained in the wide angles of the compositions and by the monumental cast of the visages. The figures and compositions are laid out in a deceptive calm, fitting the area of the relief to the rim and covering most of the ground. The reduction of a mature, three-dimensional form to one assimilated to the surface is a recurrent trait in the history of Indian art (p. 24). It marks a new beginning or else a recession into folk art.

Reliefs like those shown on Plates 6 and 7 were carved in close contiguity with others on the walls and covered the walls, or they were spaced in rhythmical sequences. The figures of these two reliefs belong to the lesser hierarchies which form the retinue and companions (sakhī) to the great gods whose images, like that of Durgā (Pl. 8), occupied the central niche on one of the faces of the temple.

The image of Durgā slaying the Buffalo Titan is not far removed in time from these two small reliefs, but its massed shadows sharpen the contours of the image and invigorate the design. The back view of the Buffalo Titan is related by its slant and by the angles of its arms and legs to the Nāga. The figures of goddess and Titan are heavy limbed in their slow-motion gestures; the masses congeal; goddess and Titan form one unit of plastic movement whose direction hovers between descent and ascent. The Titan in his defeat acts as the support of the goddess. In his surrender he accepts the fated end with an impassioned calm. This calm is conveyed by the horizontal of his wrenched head whose curves fit into and paraphrase in the horizontal the tortuous vertical of the goddess' main left arm. The agony of the Buffalo Titan is as ambiguous as is the victory of the goddess who allows her foot to rest on the hand and shoulder of the Titan, her downward glance shedding contemplative compassion upon him. An arm of the goddess droops over her raised knee with languorous elegance, while the dying Titan's arms are bent in movements of restraint and self-possession. The arms form the scale on which the combat is weighed, so that the defeated Titan, with the diagonal of his body, supports the onslaught of the goddess, and their shapes are exalted in an ascending configuration. The dynamics of this plastic mass are slow and insistent.

The buffalo's head wrenched back on the crushed, squatting, but also almost soaring male body is an Orissan version of the all-Indian theme of Durgā killing the Buffalo Titan. It is found in several images in Bhuvaneshvar, none of which surpasses the gravity and consistency of the sculpture in the Museum.

The three reliefs (carved under the Śailodbhava and Bhauma-Kara dynasties) are representative of early Orissan temple sculpture. They can be assigned to the eighth century, the two small reliefs to the early part of the century, the image of Durgā towards its end. In the eighth century, Orissan sculpture is heavy, as if a viscous sap would but slowly course through its tubular and spherical shapes. The faces of the figures have a correspondingly grave cast. It is only on the countenance of Durgā that the torpor is lifted from the lower half of the visage. The full oval with its pointed chin already belongs to Orissa, in some of the earlier figures as of the Paraśurāmeśvara temple.[47] In the coming centuries, its candour was to outstrip the gravity of the large-featured face akin to the countenance of Deccan sculpture, just as the form itself of sculpture was to leave the viscous overall plasticity which it had in common with the contemporary and earlier sculpture of the Deccan.

The image of Kārttikeya (Pl. 9) was a Pārśvadevatā on a Śiva temple of about the eleventh century. The broad spread of the body of the young god, enhanced by the width of the movement of his arms and the malleable shapes of the peacock's curved neck, of limbs and garlands of the flying celestials above (Pls. 9, 11), and of the lotus design on the base, show the orientation of the Orissan form idiom, particularly in view of the early phase of sculptures like those of the Uttareśvar temple.[48] It is at this phase that the plastic conception becomes palpable as senuous beauty, for the modelling lingers on the might of the chest as well as its adolescent feminine contours and on the narrowness of the waist as well as the delights of plastic movement that circles around the deep navel. The surging youth of the body of the god has gone into the form of this image. The artist has caressed the mystery of Kārttikeya's nature by spreading his enigmatic smile in curved planes under the width of his diademed head (Pl. 10). In faces like this from now on Orissa was to behold divinity.

Indian sculpture repeatedly, and in more than one school, passes through similar sensuous-naturalistic phases, for instance in Mathurā of the second century A.D. (Pl. 2B). But the allover plastic form of the image is constrained. The finished, detailed modelling of head and torso is not extended to the limbs, whose schematic shapes are empty of the informing breath and sap which were in the whole image, body and face, limbs and entourage of the earlier sculptures (Pl. 8). The precise details of jewelry, garment, and coiffure on and around the polished plastically animated modelling of face and chest are due, to some extent, to the material of this slab, a dark, indurated talc as soft as soapstone when quarried and hardening, on exposure to the air, to an effect of metal.

From this age onward, the images of the Pārśvadevatās were carved of this deep-green, dark stone, similar in appearance to the black steles of the images of Bengal, whose form they parallel by means of Orissan tradition. The contrast with the reddish, porous sandstone of the temple walls is striking, but originally it would have been more a contrast of colour than of texture, for the entire walls of these temples, with their sculptures, were stained red with a polished coat of iron oxide.

The—generally—dark image slabs from now onward carry their family likeness through the three centuries of the climax of Orissan temple architecture. As images of

[47] Rambach and de Golish, *op. cit.,* Pl., 67.

[48] "Kalinga Temples," Pl. XIX 1–2. The faces of the images of the Uttareśvar temple were recarved, apparently at the time of the restoration of the temple.

the major divinities, they are separated in their niches in the centre of the wall from the surrounding sculptures and are more strictly bound to the canons of proportionate measurement (tālamāna) and iconography, laid down in the priestly textbooks (śāstra). Moreover, they all appear to have come from one workshop or centre of production which supplied these images to Śaiva, Buddhist, and Saura temples throughout Orissa. With their technical smoothness goes an increasing rigour, particularly of the main, central figure of the slab, whereas the small surrounding figures are as alive in expressive movement as are the sandstone sculptures of the temple walls (Pls. 11, 13).

Within the span of a century in which the images of Kārttikeya (Pl. 9) and Khasarpaṇa Lokeśvara (Pl. 12) were carved, the luscious, surging modelled planes of the body tightened. In any profile, an impeccably controlled outline holds in check their modelling. The sensuous accentuation has become subdued and smoothed. The formerly generous cusps and indentations of the contour have been straightened into a linear, only slightly oscillating, continuity bounding the fullness of the body. Its modelling has subsided into shallow, though still sensitive, gradations of relief. The plastic conception is made to obey the conscious grip of the elegant outline. The modelling is as if restrained by an allover snugly fitting, invisible maillot. The definition of the outline is enhanced by cutting away the slab around the figure, echoing in a trefoil arch the outline of the seated god.

In the earlier image (Pl. 9), a rectangular field was cut away on either side of the figure, parallel with the rectangular outline of the slab and unrelated in its proportions to those of the figure. The trefoil around crown and head of Khasarpaṇa (Pl. 12) and the pilasters supporting this architectural feature harmonize in their proportions with the seated figure of the god. Finally, in the thirteenth century the great images of the Sun god in Koṇārak, bound in the rigour of near stereometric planes of their shape, emerge as sculpture in the round from the majestic frame of their slab which accompanies and aggrandises the effect of the image.[49]

Where the primal plastic creativeness slows down, its subsiding pulsations are caught in controlled planes and lines of increasing definition and virtuosity. The line becomes singled out from the plastic volume. Where the planes meet, thin feelerlike ridges outline and separate the once melting planes of the plastic continuum (cf. the face in Pls. 10, 11 with Pls. 12, 13). In these late phases, the small subservient figures around the image are free from the thraldom of its iconographical code and the conventions of the school that have accreted around it. In the animation of their movement and mien pulses the sap of plastic form (Pls. 13, 12). Their crowded setting is a-quiver with joy and expectation.

Before this phase (in the eleventh century), Orissan art was ripe for recep-

[49] *The Art of Indian Asia,* Pls. 371, 372.

tion of a new impact. It came from the school of Khajurāho[50] in the wake of a new architectural theme (the part-Śikharas clinging to the central Śikhara; Rājarāṇī temple) and a new zest and pointedness of sculptural form. In Mid-India, under the rule of the Candella dynasty, Nāgara architecture had attained its summit in Khajurāho of the tenth and eleventh centuries and had evolved a rarefied sculptural form. Its knife-edged subtlety, the attenuation and angularity of the tubular limbs of its figures,[51] and a geometrising of their globular shapes affected some of the sculpture of the temples in Bhuvaneshvar of the eleventh and twelfth centuries, especially of the Lingarāja and the Brahmeśvara temples. The Mithuna (Pl. 14) has some of the pointedness and sophistication of form and expression in which the Candella school excelled (cf. Pls. 31, 33).

None of the qualities, none of the trends of Orissan sculpture are forgotten in the stupendous Sun temple of Koṇārak (mid-thirteenth century). This monument carries with pristine verve, in the lateness of its style, the "summa" of Orissan sculpture. The innate Orissan, slow-flowing plasticity, its broad spread, its sensuous intensification, the sage suavity akin to that of Bengal, the zest of the Khajurāho impact—all these currents combine in a synthesis which makes the smallest detail of the carved wall bristle with a baroque virtuosity (Pl. 15). With the power over light and shade unleashed in the unending designs, carved, modelled, and undercut, a plastically propelled "naturalism" is at play in wall enhancements which have the wave for their theme (Pl. 15). Of equal conceptual immediacy is the concretion of a humorous fancy (Pl. 16), the figure of a "Deul Cāraṇī." Its function, on top of the temple spire, is compacted in its squatting shape, pressing down the gigantic tower lest the building with all the gods imaged on its walls fly up to heaven.

Apparently not from the Sun temple itself but closely related to the style of carving on the dance-hall (Nāṭa Mandir) of the Sun temple at Koṇārak is the Mithuna group (Pls. 17, 18). Its shapes are turgid with the breath and sap of plastic form locked in rapture and stillness in the closed unit of voids and encircling masses.

While Orissan temple sculpture in its earlier phase is allied to that of the Deccan, and in its later phases (Keśara-Gaṅga dynasty) becomes one of the two main branches of the Eastern school, its identity throughout the centuries is seen in the spread-out leisure of plastic form. The width of its tensions allows vibrations with their under and overtones to linger in the modelling. These vibrations convey moods steeped in the nature of their theme, whether its connotations are those of pathos (Pl. 7), humor (Pl. 16), the fatefulness of the erotic moment (Pl. 17) and its play (Pl. 14), or of the cosmic ambivalence in the configuration of Goddess and Titan (Pl. 8) or in the portrait of Kārttikeya's divinity (Pl. 9). An innate plastic conception bids the curved planes to

[50] *The Art of India,* Pl. 121.

[51] Represented on the Kandariyā and subsequent temples (*The Hindu Temple,* Pls. 15, 30, 31).

swing in all directions within the betel-leaf shape of the adolescent face (Pl. 10) and masses enlacing volumes of stone and space around a "state of union" expressed in the form of a Mithuna group (Pl. 17). The school of Orissa reached its climax in the thirteenth century in Koṇārak where all its possibilities were used and exhausted. Excepting the main figures of some of its later cult images, this school did not become "academic" as did the other leading school of Eastern Indian sculpture (that of Bihār and Bengal), judged by the majority of its cult images in stone.

BIHĀR AND BENGAL Under the Pāla and Sena dynasties, from the middle of the eighth to the end of the twelfth century, the output of the school of Bihār and Bengal was prolific. The many cult images which have been preserved must be imagined in their original setting, in temples with their walls of moulded and carved bricks, teeming with an inventiveness which the carved bricks from the temple of Pahārpur[52] show, or also the shrines that were built under Mogul rule nine hundred and a thousand years later. The stupendous wealth of form of a millennium wrought in brick has returned to the earth of which it was made. What has survived besides the images in stone are a few wood sculptures and some stone doorways and pillars and their carvings, in relief. Major figures set up near the entrance or let into the walls of the temple, like the Nāga Mithuna (Pl. 21), have also survived. It is in these—now, by the accidents of preservation, exceptional—sculptures that the genius of Pāla and Sena sculpture is revealed.

Buddhist, Viṣṇuite, and Śivaite cult images in the shape of steles were produced in great numbers, competently, according to the canon, while uninterruptedly evolving from the consolidated form of the early ninth century to its overwrought final form at the close of the twelfth century. To the outsider these sculptures offer paradigms of stylistic evolution. To the devotee they were means of contact with divinity and of a transformation of his self. Sculpture here is an "applied art," applied to the religious purpose which it helps to fulfill.

The plastic quality is consciously channelled and transmitted in the correctness of its form. Notwithstanding this controlled and directed practise of art, an uncontrollable factor is seen at work in these images, the progression of style itself. The factor of time, conveyed through form, traces its own pattern from generation to generation in the work of a school. Time itself in its inexorable pace is seen on the move in definable form through the four centuries of cult images of Bengal and Bihār. Their features are carried out in every detail conforming with the general cast of that school. The relaxed contours of the figures and pillars in the relief of "Buddha subduing the raging elephant" (Pl. 19) lead to the tempered curve of the trefoil arch above and the

[52] K. N. Dikshit, "The Temple of Pahārpur," *Archaeological Survey of India,* Memoir No. 55, Pls. XXXIX–LVII.

staid scrollwork around it. The plastic mass appears as if evenly poured into the mould of this composition of the latter part of the ninth century.

The Buddha is shown here crowned, in that body of manifestation (Sambhoga-Kāya) in which he is beheld by the elect, the Bodhisattvas,[53] who have renounced their own absorption into transcendence in order to remain and communicate to man the doctrine of the Buddha. He appears to the Bodhisattvas with crown and jewels, although clad in a monk's robe. The crown adds height to the image and by enlarging the area of the head draws greater attention to it. No rules of proportion are laid down in the textbooks which specify the height of the crown, although its varieties are classified, and it serves as a cognisance of a god. Of the three triangles of the diadem of the crown of the Buddha (Pls. 20, 19), the central triangle forms the peak of the composition, whether its symmetry is free and balanced in the distribution of weight and sculptured accents (Pl. 19) or rigid as in images of the Buddha after the tenth century (Pl. 20) when the shapes and facial features have become attenuated with dogmatic elegance.

Stylistically the Nāga Mithuna (Pl. 21) with its serpent-lithe shapes stands between the fulsome, slow plastic movement of the earlier Buddha image (Pl. 19) and the calculated refinement of the schematised shapes of the later image (Pl. 20). It has its place in the first part of the tenth century. Within the logical development of the school, the configuration of this Nāga Mithuna epitomises the qualities of the art of Bengal and Bihār. No unappeased tensions dilate and aggrandise the composure of this configuration, except in the slanted, long crescents of the brow, tremulously echoed by the lids drooping in winged, double curves.[54] In this facial zone where, according to traditional knowledge, the worlds of the senses and the intellect meet,[55] their encounter has found expression in sculptural terms (Pls. 20, 21, 23). Nowhere in Indian art outside the Pāla-Sena school of sculpture and painting has highbrow tension been answered by as vibrant a flutter of the lids. Carrying this united expression of sensual-emotional engagedness and intellectual discipline across the width of the face, the eyes of the gods, with the wings of the spirit, draw to themselves the life of sculpture. Uncanny power dwells within the lowered lids. Their upward slant imparts to the composure of the mien a feral secrecy. At a time when the gods had long ago been given their human-animal cast of form and had been revealing themselves ever anew in its

[53] P. Mus, "Le Bouddha Paré," *Bulletin de l'École Française d'Extrême Orient,* XXVIII (1928), 194, 198.

[54] The double curve of the lid stems from the Gupta schools in eastern India; cf. Sārnāth (*The Art of India,* Pl. 50).

[55] Between the brows is situated the Ājñā cakra, the subtle and invisible plexus of "command." It is here that the person merges with the universal intellect (Mahat). Here the celestial host is at his service (*Śiva-Saṃhitā,* 5, 140–41).

lineaments, mytho-plastic imagination concentrates in this school of eastern India on a physiognomical trait of the images and creates a form of the eye by which once again the more than human nature of the gods is made concrete.

The energies concentrated in the shaping of the eyes had no resonance in the modelling of Pāla images. Sculptures produced from the mid-eleventh century and under the rule of the Sena dynasty in the latter part of the eleventh to the close of the twelfth century show a progressive conventionalisation of the established types of the deities, in images such as that of the goddess Caṇḍī (Pl. 22). Straight in her upright stance as the pillar of the Universe—which she is in her principial aspect as the Great Goddess[56]—her limbs are plastically inarticulate and lifeless in their overdecorated trimness. But—the back of the slab behind her is a-flutter with curlicues of feather and cloud shapes. These are drawn into a rococo dissolution, busy around the hallowed image of the goddess. The nervous intensity which had precipitated itself into the flutter of the lids of the image now spends itself around the figures of the images in effete and overwrought detail, unable either to become form once more or to assail the rigour of the images of the divinities.

The image of Caṇḍī belongs to the eleventh century somewhere in between the images of Kārttikeya (Pl. 9) and Khasarpaṇa (Pl. 12) of the Orissa school. The pace of time left its imprint on both these schools in the sequence of styles as they transmute the traditions of each school. The rectangular slabs of the Pārśvadevatās, which have their place in the niches on the outside of the Orissa temple walls and the increasingly, as time goes on, pointed steles which were placed in the middle of the innermost sanctuary of the temples of Bihār or Bengal are similar in their successive stages of rigour but apart in the coinage of the sensualism of this late phase in spite of earlier contacts and similarities. Sensualism or else "naturalism" here means a tactile rendering of the body as the container of breath and the life sap. Its shape here is less formed as the visible limit thrown up by the indwelling movement itself than as the palpable substance deposited by that movement and touched by the sensibility of the sculptor. In Orissa (Pls. 9, 12), this naturalism gave richness to the modelling; in Bengal, at the end (Pl. 24), it arrested in descriptive details the modelling of the fulsome trunk of the figures. Sensualism had also contributed towards the form of the Pāla school of the ninth century (Pl. 19), when the figure, as a whole, appeared fleshy in the roundedness of the thighs and fullness of the chest. In the twelfth century (Pl. 24), schematic shapes below the waist and burgeoning shapes above the girdle of the image of Sūrya, the sun god, are connected by a hard contour. Frizzy zig-zags of fluttering scarves link the planes of the elaborate theophany of this stele. The brows of Sūrya are

[56] In the Hymn of the Goddess (*Devī sūkta*) of the *Ṛig Veda* (10.125.7), Vāc, as the Great Goddess, sings of herself: "My origin is in the waters, in the sea . . . with the crown of my head I touch the sky."

wrinkled in scallops over bulging, wide-open eyes true to the iconographic prescription of rendering furor.[57]

The sculptor, in his supererogation to give complete exposition to the nature of the deity, followed the iconography of Sūrya in all its details. The figures are symmetrically balanced in the staggered planes of this slab. All the requisites are staged in their allotted places so that the centred image of the Sun god rises in fierce majesty. The marshalling of this theophany in the space and on the surface of the stele has grandeur. It is sealed by the medallion of the encircled horse in the middle of the pedestal (Pl. 25). No power drives the chariot of the god. The power of the sculptor is spent in shaping the towering presence of the Sun god and in the organisation and frilly elaboration of this theme (Pl. 24).

Sculpture of the Eastern school in Bengal under the Sena dynasty came to an end about the year 1200 when the plastic flow stagnated, unable to absorb a nervous excitement which found its visual outlet in crowding frills around sculptural embodiments of iconographic prescriptions. At that time the Muslims, under Muhammed Khalji, wrested Bengal from Lakṣmanasena in the early years of the thirteenth century. Orissa was spared a similar fate and soared with the unfinished Sun temple of Koṇārak to the peak of Indian art. To the great master who built this temple and carved some of its sculptures, all the resources of the Orissan tradition lay open. He gathered and infused them with his vision and had to leave parts of the work in the hands of his school. The work of the school shows that it belongs to the thirteenth century, when in Orissa, too, the style had come to the end of its possibilities. Henceforward, the plastic vitality of Indian sculpture recedes and is superseded by static configurations imposed on its context.

Schools of the Midland and of Rājasthān

The other schools of northern India had coined their final plastic features in the eleventh century with the last subtleties of their respective traditions. No single centre or local school, however, except Bengal-Bihār, Orissa, and Rājasthān, is known at the present in the continuity of its work during the preceding centuries. Much has been destroyed, and not all the remains have been collected.

In the Vārāṇasī-Sārnāth school, in the Gupta age during the fifth and sixth centuries, a rarefied type of the image of Buddha was created which became a universal symbol of Buddhahood. The pure, merging planes of the Gupta images with their infinitesimal vibrations of the surface represent a sublimation of Indian plasticity. The

[57] *Viṣṇudharmottara,* III. 37. 9–15.

perfection of this form was to underlie northern Indian sculpture for the next half-millennium.

In the eleventh century, a figure of a dancing Gaṇa from Vārāṇasī (Pl. 26) has the flexibility of modelling which this school kept supple even where, in more relaxed curving planes, this figure is distended with a brooding satiety. The dancing body is topped by a half-complacent, half-scurrilous mien which has the face for its shape. This is not a case of an ordinary face carrying expression. Rather a complex state of being together with the awareness of its being have created the lineaments and proportions of a face, where they reverberate from the modelling of eyes and mouth, cheeks and curly locks.

A similar degree of psychological awareness and intellectual assessment of this awareness is formed in the head of a Śiva image from the vicinity of Allahabad (Pl. 28). The face is young and compassionate, knowing and terrifying in the smoothed planes of its broad forehead and the relaxed contour of its cheeks.

Faces like these belong to the tenth and eleventh centuries in the schools of sculpture which extended in a narrow belt from Vārāṇasī over Khajurāho (Pls. 28, 35) and into northern Rājasthān. Faces like these, and the bodies that carried them, are engaged in a dialogue with themselves, in terms of the plastic substance of sculpture. States of being, knowing, and savouring themselves are the subject of these schools of Indian temple sculpture (Pls. 26, 35). Because their plastic form is the created visual equivalent of the felt movement of the breath and sap of life, it carries at a given stage —the tenth to eleventh century—of the sculptor's conscious awareness the play of emotions and the movements of thought as they are brought forth on the face and the body. As spontaneously as they well up in their equivocal tensions they are impressed on the plastic substance. A smile saddens the lips over which it passes (Pl. 36), eyes meditate on the life which the mouth savours (Pl. 35), cheeks are like petals (Pl. 28), and noses have aquiline sharpness (Pl. 33). Because Indian sculpture is the form of the "subtle body" (sūkṣma śarīra) of man, the temper of feeling together with the potential of thought are merged with its substance. Where passion or beatitude (Pl. 36) or any intense emotion or realisation is to be rendered, the plastic plenum reverberates in its entire range.

Because the vibrancy of life as it is felt and known in and through the body— and not the perishable shape of the body itself—is the theme of Indian sculpture, its form is capable of expressing all measures of life from the sensual to the transcendental plane.

The sculptures of these schools speak the dialogue of existence while embodying states of being. Their volumes, planes, and curves convey multiple resonances even in marginal compositions like that of the conversation of two disciples (Pl. 27). Here the dialogue embodied in the figure of each of the two boys goes on while they argue and deliberate in a world of their own in the deep shadow of a roof whose height is appropriate to the seated group within the flanking pilasters.

If the Sun temple of Koṇārak is the "summa" of Orissan art, the sculptures of the temples of Khajurāho have this significance for the Mid-Indian belt which extended from Vārāṇasī to Rājasthān. The transitions in form from one centre to the next are gradual and, at times, impalpable. While the formal quality of the Gaṇa from Vārāṇasī (Pl. 26) cannot be found amongst sculptures from the centres west of Khajurāho, a relief like the group of the two boys from the vicinity of Allahabad (Pl. 27) would not be unexpected among similar carvings in Khajurāho. Moreover, there is as much variation among the faces of the gods in Khajurāho (Pls. 29, 31, 32, 35) as between them and the Śiva head from the vicinity of Allahabad (Pl. 28) or the face of an image of Nirṛiti from the vicinity of Aligarh (p. 91). But the sculptures of Khajurāho itself are not all variations of only one formal mode. They represent two types of form—the one traditional and at its height in the tenth century,[58] the other new and at its height in the eleventh century.[59]

The traditional form is burdened by its own mass, at times (Pls. 30, 32), and opaque if compared with the flow and flexibility in the modelling of the Gaṇa from Vārāṇasī (Pl. 26).[60] This traditional form, however, flows with a melody (Pl. 37) and is stirred by subtleties as delicate and dedicated as surrender to God and beatitude will communicate to the movement of the hands and the countenance of a goddess (Pl. 36).

The "new form" is trenchant in the vehemence of a movement that spaces the traditional shapes in angles pointed with activity. This new form comes into its own when it assails the plastic mass itself until its convex curves become concave (cf. Pl. 34), until its plasticity obeys an outline which is as taut as the curve of a tightly drawn bow and yields profiles as straight as an arrow. The long-limbed, angular, and opulent figures (not represented in the Museum collections) in their torsions on the temple walls of Khajurāho[61] represent this new form. It occurs somewhat earlier than the eleventh century in western India, in Rājasthān,[62] and it became the leading form in the marble temples of Western India from the eleventh into the fifteenth century.

Of the schools south of those extending from Vārāṇasī into Rājasthān, two are represented in the Museum. The Haihaya school whose masterworks are the images of the sixty-four Yoginīs of the eighth and tenth centuries in Bheraghat[63] near Jabalpur,

[58] Krishna Deva, "The Temples of Khajuraho in Central India," *Ancient India,* 15 (1959), Pl. XXXVIII B; *The Hindu Temple,* Pls. XI, XIV.

[59] *Ibid.,* Pls. XV, XXIII.

[60] See also the dancing Gaṇas in Khajurāho, Pl. XXXIII, Fig. 2, *Journal of the Indian Society of Oriental Art,* I (1933).

[61] *The Hindu Temple,* Pls. 13, 15, 30. *The Art of India,* Pl. 122.

[62] *The Art of India,* Pls. 117, 118.

[63] *The Art of India,* Pls. 127, 128. R. D. Banerji, "The Haihayas of Tripuri," *Archaeological Survey of India,* Memoir No. 23.

is shown by two Jaina sculptures of the later date (p. 94). This school is capable of expressing piercing intensity in bold, at times crowded, volumes and derives from them its unmistakable identity. Where the record of such tensions has become the routine of the school, the sculptures have an obtuse Haihaya physiognomy.

The other school is the Paramāra school of ancient Mālwā, with centres in Ujjain, Udayapur, Gyāraspur, and Candrāvatī, although Candrāvatī is situated in the state of Rājasthān. In these sculptures, one's eye is made to halt on a mouth (Pl. 44), a belt, or arm (Pl. 45). The single sculptural configuration is not a vibrant whole of infinitesimal transitions of modelling, but has its integrity in the disposition of the weight of the component parts (Pl. 47). Their volumes are articulate, in depth, zoned, and thus connected in the compositional movement. Their form is compact—the linear movement, a reasoned arrangement. The figures, some of whose eyes have the pupils marked (Pl. 44), look out on this world, steadfast and disillusioned. The frequently long, heavy oval of the faces, the mighty brows, and the mouth unsmiling, even where its corners are drawn upwards (Pls. 44, 46), express self-possessed composure. Notwithstanding the more static character of its volumes, the Mālwā school of sculpture achieves its form by means of the plastic mass.

In Rājasthān, as in Orissa, stylistic changes can be followed over the centuries, from the earlier (eighth and ninth centuries) in Abaneri and Osia[64] to the later sculptures of Harṣagiri and Kiradu (tenth to twelfth century). But the main Orissan monuments are centred in one major area, whereas the several phases of Rājasthān sculpture belong to sites as far apart as Harṣagiri, the "mountain of joy," north of Jaipur (Pls. 38, 39), and Kiradu (eleventh to twelfth century) to the west of Jodhpur (Pls. 40–43). The sculptures from the several sites of Rājasthān from the eighth to the twelfth century are sprightly, correlating delicacies of modelling with exquisite shapes of jewelry, weapons, scarves, and flowers, and, in fact, with all that touches and surrounds the modelled, breathing shapes of their figures in ever varied configurations, such as the thin sword-and-bow shapes interknit with the warrior-youths (Pl. 39), or the more ponderous theme of tree and lute (vīṇā) interwoven with the goddess and her ministering dwarfs (Pl. 38). The compositions sparkle with crisp shapes. In their spirited contact, as in Kiradu (Pls. 43, 41), the scarves, for example, not only enhance but cincture so as to hold and prevent from erupting the valour (Pl. 43) or youth (Pl. 41) of a figure. This is bodied forth in curved planes like those of figures in Khajurāho,[65] to whose shapes, however, these garments merely cling.[66]

In the later part of the tenth and the first half of the eleventh century a new zestful

[64] For Abaneri, see *Lalitkalā*, I–II (1955–56), Pls. LII–LXIII; and for Osia, *The Art of India* (1955) Pls. 115–116.

[65] Cf. *The Hindu Temple*, Pl. XXIII.

[66] *Ibid.*, Pls. XX, XXI, XXIII.

and incisive line disciplined intellectually, and accentuated emotionally, the classical rotundities of sculpture in Rājasthān and central India. With critical and dialectical finesse it gripped the tensions between the will and the emotions on the one hand and states of vegetative or mystically realised being on the other. This new expressiveness of form found its way also to Orissa, where it was absorbed by the placid volumes of that Eastern school.

When by the close of the twelfth century sculpture in Bengal had come to the end of its stylistic evolution, the conquest of Bengal by the Muslims coincided with and outwardly put an end to a form already in exhaustion. When Muslim rule became consolidated in India, Indian sculpture, though under a shadow, continued creating new form. After the thirteenth century, the new element, on the negative side, is a bleakness, void of plasticity; while on the positive side, it is a static, cubic solidity. It is seen in two of its final versions, both from Jaipur, the four-faced Liṅga from Sāmbhar Lake (Pl. 49) and the head from Amber (Pl. 50). The former reduces the face to planear dimensions of archaic symmetry which adhere to the stereometric shape of the Liṅga. The latter partly translates into and partly assimilates plastic volume to stereometric shape. In these translations, the traditional context is fully understood. There is, then, no surprise if it is activated again in the plasticity of a wall figure (Pl. 51) wearing a necklace of the Mogul period, whereas the torso is modelled according to Indian tradition, from the temple sculptures of more than five hundred years before. The difference due to this distance in time in the form of this sculpture is, however, not greater than the difference between Cambodian sculpture of the sixth and seventh centuries and the contemporary Indian schools.

The resurgence of plastic form in a changed India, which had absorbed once more—as it had done in the early centuries of the Christian era—the impact of political and cultural invasions from the north, proves the vitality of this creative substance.

Chambā, a North Indian Centre

A different story is told by the art of the (former) small Himālayan mountain state of Chambā. In the Museum collection (Pl. 48) this art is shown in two of its chapters in the shape of perforated reliefs of the same date (about the eleventh century) and probably from the same building. They represent two of the ten incarnations of Viṣṇu and served as images in the wall of a temple where they also functioned as windows. The slab with the Rāmacandra Avatar (p. 100) shows a last and faint reflex on Indian soil of classical Western art. The classical art of the West had been received by the school of Gandhāra-Afghanistan (p. 52), from which some of its features—particularly of the face—travelled, took root in Kashmir, and finally branched off into the high mountain country of Chambā.[67] On the whole, however, the panel with Rāmacandra (p. 100) shows a local adaptation of contemporary form as practised in centres in the Indian plains. In the Fish Avatar panel (Pl. 48), the local tradition of Chambā is seen to advantage. It is a folk art with many extra-Indian affiliations into which the Indian gods and symbols are drawn. They have shed most of their Indian form; they have been squared and planed; and in this reduced state, they fit into a frame replete with the ancient, sacred symbols of the fish and the tree and pillar of life.

South India

While the art of the Southern Deccan is shown in one example only (p. 101), South Indian stone sculpture in one of its later phases is included in the Museum collection by an image of Gaṇeśa (Pl. 54) and, in its architectural context, it is represented in the Museum by a pillared temple hall from Madura of the sixteenth century (Pls. 55, 56).[68] At this phase, the theme of a large figure and of an architectural unit, the pillar, is forced into contiguity without dynamic coherence. If the sculptural form of this configuration appears depleted of vital substance, the spacing of the figured pillars with their heavy bracket capitals makes the entire hall a sculpted interior.

The space of its nave is bounded by the curving slant of the pillar figures and their bracket capitals whose arc seems to spring from the low base of the pillar, giving vertical backing to each of the standing figures. The figures bend forward into the nave, their high crowns reach up to the bracket capitals which support a flat ceiling. The ascending arc of these superimposed carvings is virtually flung across the flat ceiling and rests on the corresponding figured pillar in the opposite row flanking the nave of the temple hall. The length of the nave is filled with arched rhythms of carved space. In their chiaroscuro the carved figures come to life. They bend over and conduct the pilgrim and the visitor to the small door of the sanctuary.

The South Indian metal images in the Museum date from the thirteenth (Pl. 52) and fourteenth (Pl. 53) to the eighteenth or nineteenth century (Pl. 57). These images, meant to be carried in procession, are cast in the round. Stereotyped in their specific South Indian form, they follow prototypes which were perfected in the tenth and eleventh centuries and are receptacles of the tradition that had given plastic form to the breath and sap of life.

[67] H. Goetz, *The Early Wooden Temples of Chamba* (Leiden, 1956), pp. 111–12.
[68] W. Norman Brown, *A Pillared Hall from a Temple at Madura,* Figs. 2–25.

Catalogue

FIRST CENTURY B.C.— CA. FIFTH CENTURY A.D.

1. WORSHIPPER *Fragment of railing post, Bhuvaneshvar, Orissa, ca. first century* B.C.

(PLATE 1)

The figure shown in front view has its hands folded in front of the chest in the gesture of obeisance (añjali mudrā). Its long, full, oval face is framed by hair with incised, radiating lines. It covers the ears down to the ear ornament of three heavy rings (cf. A. K. Coomaraswamy, *La Sculpture de Bhārhut,* Pl. XV). The wide-open eyes framed in ridge-shaped lids fill the width of the face, below a high forehead. A long, fleshy nose and full lips distinguish this large-featured face with its more detailed modelling from similar figures in Bhārhut. The figure wears a necklace of two rows of beads, armlets of three and bracelets of five rings. A sash with horizontal, parallel lines indicating folds is knotted in the middle, at a distance below the navel.

The navel is always clearly shown. According to Yoga, the universal and vital life force (Kuṇḍalinī Śakti) which regulates the movement of the breath is coiled around the navel (*Triśikhī Brāhmaṇa Upaniṣad,* 62–64).

The ground of the relief slants slightly towards the figure which fills its width.

56.75.1

Published: Stella Kramrisch, "A Stone Relief From a Kaliṅga Railing," *Indian Antiquary,* LX (1931), 89, Pl. 2. *Philadelphia Museum Bulletin,* LII (1957), 32.
Buff sandstone. Top broken; slightly battered 13¾″ x 8½″

MATHURĀ (KUṢĀṆA DYNASTY)

2. SŪRYA, THE SUN GOD *Mathurā, Uttar Pradesh, second to third century* A.D.

Relief slab. A squatting figure, clad in a long-sleeved tunic, holds an object against the right shoulder; the left arm rests on the left knee; the left hand clasps a sword attached to the belt. The figure wears earrings, necklace, and a low, close-fitting Tocharian(?) cap. A nimbus (*śiraścakra*) is carved behind the head.

31.60.20

Gift of N. M. Heeramaneck
Buff Sikri sandstone. Weathered; surface worn 6$^{5}/_{16}$″ x 6″

3. HEAD OF TĪRTHANKARA *Mathurā, Uttar Pradesh, ca. fourth century.*

The head of the Jain Saviour is covered with curls.

17.167

Gift of Paul Mallon
Cf. *Pennsylvania Museum Bulletin,* XXVII (1932), 123–25.
Red Sikri sandstone. Battered 10″ x 8¼″

4. TĪRTHANKARA *Mathurā, third century.*

Head and bust only; large, circular halo (śiraścakra) with starlike centre; scallops between rays along perimeter of inner circle. Scallop and beads on outer rim.

31.60.8

Gift of N. M. Heeramaneck
Red mottled Sikri sandstone. Weathered 7″ x 6½″

5. HEAD OF AN ACOLYTE OF THE BUDDHA *Mathurā, Uttar Pradesh, second century* A.D.

(PLATE 2a)

A quilted cap with crest on the left closely fits the head of the long, schematically treated face. Part of the slab of the image is preserved on the right.

56.75.5

Red mottled Sikri sandstone. 7¼″ x 6¾″

6. HEAD OF A ROYAL PERSONAGE *Mathurā, Uttar Pradesh, second century* A.D.

(PLATE 2b)

The small-featured, moustached, round face is surmounted by the fantail crest of the turban which had a bird (suparṇa) ornament in the middle. The head is carved in the round with one end of the turban hanging over to the neck. The large ear ornaments are indistinct.

56.75.4

Red mottled Sikri sandstone. Top damaged; weathered 7⅝″ x 5″

7. WORSHIPPING YAKṢĪ *Fragment of railing post, Mathurā, Uttar Pradesh, second half, first century.*

(PLATE 3)

The Yakṣī, whose hands are folded (añjali mudrā), wears a long shawl over her shoulders indicating that she is engaged in worship. A long, diaphanous skirt (āprapadīna) is held in position by a hip-girdle (mekhalā) of four bead strings and a clasp in front. A string of beads (ekāvalī) round her neck, another dangling between her breasts, armlets, a bracelet of many rings, ending with a twisted bracelet, and ear-plugs are the ornaments. The hair is parted on both sides of a low bun, covering part of the forehead; a leafy or flowering twig, carved in low relief, is seen to the left of the face.

The diaphanous skirt of this life- and love-promoting genie shows her generative organ. The long ends of the shawl, with their folds in parallel lines, are carved at a slant to the figure.

56.75.2

Published: *Philadelphia Museum Bulletin*, LII (1957), 33.
Red mottled Sikri sandstone. Nose battered 11$\frac{45}{16}$″ x 6$\frac{5}{16}$″

8. YAKṢA AND ATTENDANT *Mathurā, Uttar Pradesh, second century.*

Relief slab with standing figure, the right hand raised to the shoulder holding an indistinct object. The left hand rests on the hip. The figure wears a long shawl whose one end passes over the left wrist. The loincloth is folded in front and touches the ground between the feet. A standing dwarf Yakṣa attendant carries a heavy object in his raised hands.

31.60.12

Gift of N. M. Heeramaneck
Red mottled Sikri sandstone. Nose battered 11⅙″ x 5$\frac{13}{16}$″

9. YAKṢA *Mathurā, Uttar Pradesh, second century.*

Relief slab. The squatting, naked, pot-bellied figure holds a club (lakuṭa) in the raised right; the lowered left holds a goblet. The figure wears a low, pointed headgear, earrings, and necklace.

31.60.26

Gift of N. M. Heeramaneck
Sikri sandstone. Abrased 8 7/16″ x 4 7/8″

10. YAKṢA *Mathurā, Uttar Pradesh, third century.*

The figure (cf. 31.60.26) wears a turban, a scarf over the shoulders, and holds a casketlike object against the chest. The drapery below the naked belly is similar to that of an image of Sarasvatī, dated in the year 54, i.e., 232 A.D. (acc. to J. E. van Lohuizen de Leeuw, *The Scythian Period,* p. 288, Fig. 59).

31.60.2

Gift of N. M. Heeramaneck
Cream Sikri sandstone. Defaced 11½″ x 6⅜″

11. FRAGMENT OF RAILING POST *Mathurā, Uttar Pradesh, second century.*

(PLATE 4)

The upper panel shows two bullocks emerging from the gate of a fort. An accessory defence tower is on the right. In the lower panel, the rearing bullocks, shown in back view, storm away through a narrow mountain pass while men or monkeys, above on the left, on the rocks, eagerly watch the spectacle.

The scene has an architectural frame, consisting of pillars with an āmalaka shape, surmounted by a winged sphinx carved on the block-shaped capital. A sur-capital supports a vaulted roof-shape with two dormer windows (gavākṣa). On the back of the post is the torso of a Yakṣinī (cf. 56.75.2).

57.122.1

Anonymous gift
Red mottled Sikri sandstone. Weathered 16½″ x 8⅞″

12. FLYING DEVA *Mathurā, Uttar Pradesh, second century.*

Part of larger image. The celestial carries offerings and wears a turban, ornaments, and scarf. Flowing drapery accompanies the flying movement of the Deva.

31.60.3

Gift of N. M. Heeramaneck
Red Sikri sandstone. Weathered 8 3/16″ x 7⅜″

13. BEARDED FIGURE WEARING CONICAL CAP *Mathurā, ca. second century(?).*

Head and bust only. Right arm raised to shoulder. Low arch of slab incised with parallel vertical lines.

31.60.23

Gift of N. M. Heeramaneck
Red mottled sandstone. Weathered; face abrased 4½″ x 3½″

MATHURĀ (GUPTA DYNASTY)

14. HEAD OF DEVĪ *Mathurā, ca. fifth century.*

The hair is dressed in a flat bun on the crown of the head.

31.60.14

Red Sikri sandstone. Weathered, battered
7¾″ x 5$\frac{3}{16}$″

15. NĀGA KING AND QUEEN *Mathurā, ca. sixth century.*

Image carved in the round. The Nāga standing in tribhaṅga (triple bend), with right hand raised towards his serpent hood, holds a goblet in his left against his chest. The Nāginī stands straight (samapādasthānaka), her right hand raised towards the arm of the Nāga, her left hand rests on the hip. She holds an indistinct object in each hand. The Nāga wears a flat headgear with triangular peak; the Nāginī has a bun at the top of her head. Both wear round earrings (kuṇḍala); long shawls cross their legs below the knee. The shawl of the queen is draped over her left arm. They also wear loincloths whose ends, gathered in front, are pendant between the legs. At the back a many-hooded serpent accompanies the human shape of the Nāga and spreads his hoods like a halo around the head of the Nāga. A fewer-hooded serpent's head surrounds the head of the queen.

56.75.3

Red Sikri sandstone. Abrased; legs broken; right arm of Nāga, hood of Nāginī battered
8$\frac{1}{16}$″ x 5⅛″

GANDHĀRA (KUṢĀṆA DYNASTY)

16. HEAD OF BUDDHA *Find-place unknown, Gandhāra, Pakistan, ca. early second century.*

The face shows moustache and ūrṇā. The long wavy hair is gathered in a top knot. (Cf. Harald Ingholt, *Gandhāran Art in Pakistan,* Fig. 73; *The Scythian Period,* Figs. 5–8.)

55.86.21

Bequest of Fiske and Marie Kimball
Dark-gray schist. Forehead slightly damaged
7⅛″ x 4½″

17. HEAD OF BODHISATTVA MAITREYA *Swāt Valley, Gandhāra, Pakistan, ca. third century.*

The full, long oval of the face with the symmetry of the large, idealised features is set off against the wavy masses of flowing locks. They are tied in "krobylos" fashion above the diadem. (Cf. *Gandhāran Art,* Figs. 306, 307; *The Scythian Period,* Fig. 18.)

21.38.5

Black schist. Tip of nose chipped 13¾″ x 9⅝″

18. THE GREAT DEPARTURE *Gandhāra, Pakistan, ca. second century.*

Fragment from drum of a stūpa. The Bodhisattva Siddhārtha, nimbate and on horseback, has come out of the city gate of Kapilavastu. Two youths carrying lances(?) over their left shoulders walk in front of the horse. They represent the Śākya youths who guarded the gates of Kapilavastu and could not prevent the Buddha-to-be from leaving the city. (Cf. A. Foucher, *Les Bas Réliefs Gréco-Bouddhiques de Gandhāra,* p. 356; cf. *Gandhāran Art,* Figs. 48, 49, 51.)

The scene is flanked by pilasters. To the left, another scene is shown in part only. A garland bearer and a tree indicate "Siddhārtha's exchange of clothes with the hunter."

6.1940.6

Dark grey schist. Faces of three figures destroyed 5¼″ x 12¼″

19. HEAD OF BUDDHA *Taxila or Peshawar, Gandhāra, Pakistan, fourth to fifth century.*

29.144.4

Stucco. Nose slightly battered 3⅞″ x 2¼″

20. HEAD OF BODHISATTVA *Findplace unknown, Gandhāra, fourth century.*
(PLATE 5a)

The placid, compassionate face has its broad forehead bound by a diadem set with flowers. An ūrṇā-like disk is raised in the middle of the forehead between the eyebrows. The ear ornament has a scalloped rim. (Cf. *Gandhāran Art,* Fig. 557.)

22.49.1

Gift of Charles H. Ludington
Published: *Pennsylvania Museum Bulletin,* XVIII (November, 1922), 4.
Stucco. Headgear, right ear damaged; traces of red pigment on lips, lids, hair, ears, diadem 4″ x 2 15/16″

21. HEAD OF BODHISATTVA *Findplace unknown, Afghanistan, fifth century.*
(PLATE 5b)

The dreamy candour of the classical face is enlivened by the modelling of the corners of the mouth. The wavy hair on the head and on the conical "uṣṇīṣa"-like crest is rendered by elliptical depressions. A fillet binds the forehead and allows the hair to fall behind the elongated ears with ear-plugs.

39.19.1

Gift of Mrs. Charles Wheeler
Stucco. Traces of red pigment 4¼″ x 2 11/16″

22. HEAD OF BODHISATTVA *Gandhāra, fifth century.*

29.144.1

Stucco. Top of headgear broken; battered, abrased 9⅞″ x 6⅜″

23. HEAD OF A WARRIOR *Taxila or Peshawar, Gandhāra, second century.*

The moustached face with bulging eyes looks upward. The open mouth shows the teeth. A helmet covers the wavy hair.

29.144.2

Stucco. Traces of red pigment on hair, brows, and moustache; nose broken 7⅞″ x 5″

24. HEAD OF A WARRIOR *Taxila or Peshawar, Gandhāra, second century.*

The haggard face with sunk, wide-open eyes, large moustache, and wind-blown hair is impressionistically modelled. (Cf. Sir John Marshall, *Taxila,* Pl. 160c.)

29.144.5

Stucco. Nose battered 2 9/16″ x 2 9/16″

25. HEAD OF LAY WOMAN *Taxila or Peshawar, Gandhāra, ca. fifth century.*

The flowing, neat hair is indicated by rows of schematic, impressed crescents.

29.144.3

Stucco. Top of head damaged 6 13/16″ x 4½″

26. FOREPART OF A LION *Taxila or Peshawar, ca. fifth century.*

The pug-nosed head is shown with open mouth and lolling tongue. (Cf. *Gandhāran Art,* Figs. 576, 577.)

29.144.7

Stucco. Traces of red pigment on tongue; one leg broken 5⅛" x 4½"

27. HEAD OF A LION *Taxila or Peshawar, ca. fifth century.*

Cf. 29.144.7

29.144.6

Stucco. 2⅝" x 2¼"

* * *

28. TORSO OF YAKṢA *Find-place unknown, Northern India, ca. fifth century.*

The powerfully modelled, seated body has the left leg tucked under its loincloth; the left arm rests on the knee.

31.60.10

Gift of N. M. Heeramaneck
Terra cotta. Right leg and arm missing 6⅝" x 5 1/16"

ORISSA (ŚAILODBHAVA TO KEŚARA AND GAṄGA DYNASTIES)

29. WORSHIPPING NĀGA IN LOTUS POND *Bhuvaneshvar, Orissa, early eighth century.*

(PLATE 6)

Rhizome and stalk of the lotus are coalesced; buds and leaves spring from nodules. This ancient convention (Bhārhut, first century B.C.) here fills the panel in low relief from the right lower corner upwards. The pilaster on the left shows in its three sections the following symbols: half-lotus rosette and brimming vase (pūrṇa ghaṭa); face of glory (kīrttimukha) and scrollwork in the middle section; at the top a half lotus.

56.75.42

Reddish coarsely grained sandstone. 10⅝" x 11 3/8"

30. SAKHĪ *Bhuvaneshvar, Orissa, early eighth century.*

(PLATE 7)

This "companion" rests her right hand on her right hip. The enhancement of the right hip and the bend of the face in profile to the right make an unusual "bhaṅga" or contrapost in which the figure appears to bend over itself. The figure wears a close-fitting veil, bead necklace, and circular earring, armlet(?), and bracelet on the right arm; a shawl(?) is slung over the left arm. Part of object in left hand indistinct.

56.75.8

Published: *Journal of the Indian Society of Oriental Art,* LI (1936), Pl. XVIII, Fig. 2.
Buff sandstone. Lower part of panel broken; weathered, rim battered 4 13/16" x 3⅝"

31. DURGĀ KILLING THE BUFFALO TITAN *Bhuvaneshvar, Orissa, late eighth century.*

(PLATE 8)

Image from central niche of temple wall. The Buffalo Titan through practising incredible austerities had acquired invincible strength. The gods could not defeat him. They breathed the fiery energies (tejas) of their wrath from their mouths, in one mighty fire. Out of it arose the Great Goddess in whom are embodied the several energies of all the gods (*Mārkaṇḍeya Purāṇa,* 82, 84). As the embodied totality of primordial energy, the Great Goddess defeats the Buffalo Titan.

The goddess has placed her right foot on the right palm and shoulder of the Buffalo Titan, shown in back view. She stands on the stretched left leg behind the Titan, her body being bent in the waist, towards the left. The eight arms of the goddess hold, beginning from the uppermost right hand: sword, three-pronged spear or trident, the adamantine weapon (vajra?) and arrow, the jaw of the buffalo, serpent, bow, and shield. With her main arms, the goddess defeats the Titan. The other arms with their weapons amplify her presence and illustrate her glory. The goddess wears a broad chignon, diadem, and corkscrew locks in front of her beaded halo. Her ornaments include two different earrings; a triple necklace with long pendant between the breasts; a waist chain attached to the pendant; a heavy, tight chain as hip-girdle; armlets; various bracelets; and an anklet. Her neck and also her waist are carved in parallel folds; the latter are signs of beauty (trivali), but they are also marks of the style or date of the sculpture. The hem of the long loincloth is carved above the girdle, below the navel, and above the foot. The Buffalo Titan wears a tight, short-sleeved, cuirasse-like bodice and beaded straps from shoulders to waist; armlets; wristlets; a chain hip-belt over his loincloth (dhotī). His left arm rests on his knee; the hand is raised as support of the goddess and holds a looped cloth or sling; the right hand, with the dagger slipped under the belt, rests on the hip. The small shape of the lion on his left—the vehicle of the goddess—mauls the bent knee of the Titan. His right leg is raised from the knee.

The downward thrust of the movement of the goddess is conveyed by the concave curve of her left arm and the convex and compressed curve of her thigh. Their pincerlike volumes meet, and their thrust is held by the horizontal of the buffalo's jaw, on which rests the hand of the goddess. The long, sensitive fingers hold the Titan's buffalo jaw with effortless determination.

Whereas the profile of the right side of the Titan completes the curve of the goddess' left arm, his left profile shows him still resisting with an upward thrust, as if carrying and raising the goddess who stabs him.

The ambivalence of movement and emotion shown in this sculpture is expressed in the *Mārkaṇḍeya Purāṇa* where it is said that the goddess destroys the Titans for their own happiness, so that slain by her hand they might go to heaven. The goddess destroys in order to liberate.

(Cf., a more elegant, somewhat later and less adequate version of the same theme from the Vaitāl Deul, Bhuvaneshvar, p. 47, note.)

The lowermost part of this relief was carved on a separate stone.

56.75.7

Published: *Philadelphia Museum Bulletin,* LII (1957), 30.
Red sandstone. Traces of red pigment on face; top defaced, spear damaged, face slightly battered 2′ 3½″ x 1′ 4¹⁵⁄₁₆″

32. KĀRTTIKEYA *Puri, Orissa, eleventh century.*

(PLATES 9–11)

The rectangular image slab was fitted into the central niche of the west face of a Śiva temple.

Kārttikeya is shown as an eternal adolescent. He was brought up by the six Pleiades (Kṛttikā). He was born from the seed of Śiva —the ascetic—in order to lead the army of the gods in their battle with the Titans. His mission is similar to that of Durgā, but he is not shown in combat. He stands serenely in dvibhaṅga (double bend) in front of his vehicle, the peacock; his right hand held a javelin; his left rests on a cock. The peacock, the bird of immortality, is traditionally the killer of serpents. Cosmologically the serpent is a symbol of the cycle of the year and of recurrent time. In killing the serpent, the peacock annihilates time. The cock, who crows before sunrise, is a symbol of solar energy—from which arise the cycles of the year and of time. The cock is carved above the small figure of a woman. She is Devasenā, the consort of Kārttikeya. The two birds of Kārttikeya are symbols of two aspects of the god. Kārttikeya, whose name is also Guha, the mysterious, ever remains a boy, and he remains single; as Lord of immortality, he has conquered the Titan and the serpent power of Desire, and he has the peacock for his vehicle. Where, however, he holds the cock, there is the realm of time. Under its wings and raising her right hand in adoration (vandana) is the small figure of Devasenā.

Richly bejewelled, nimbate, Kārttikeya wears his hair in three looped meshes (śikhaṇḍaka) characteristic of boyhood. The pearl and gold diadem around the flower-wreathed head is flanked by flowerlike ruffles passed across a ring and with golden pins, above the ears. Leaves of the aśoka tree are affixed to it; they surround the ears with their circular ear-plugs; cork-screw locks fall to the shoulders. A double bead string encircles the neck; another double bead string for the tiger-claw necklace (vyāghraṇakha) rests on the chest and is like the śikhaṇḍaka appropriate for Kārttikeya, the boy. A long, twisted garland of flowers and beads (vanamālā) over the left shoulder adds its curves to those of the body, above a scarf whose lines across the chest indicate folds. The short loincloth (kaupīna) is similarly shown and also the sash around the thighs. A long pendant hangs from the buckle of the hip-belt with its bells. Armlets and bracelets of all the figures are of the usual types.

Flying "knowledge-holding" spirits (Vidyādhara) (Pl. 11) move towards the god, bringing garlands as offerings. Their long, straight hair is gathered in a mango-shaped chignon at the back of the head. Male and female, they wear boots (cf. Pls. 24–25).

The base is filled with a lotus rhizome carrying a large, double lotus as pedestal (mahāṃbujapīṭha) for the god, a small one for the goddess, and a lotus with one row of petals only for the peacock.

The slab is cut away, leaving a rectangle of space against which the figure of Kārttikeya stands out.

The rippling modelling of the torso and, particularly, the face (10) belongs to the form physiognomy of Orissan sculpture as conceived from the time of the Mukteśvar temple onward. The slightly pointed halo is fringed with flamelike scrolls.

56.75.14

Published: *Journal of the Indian Society of Oriental Art,* II (1934), Pl. XIX, Fig. 2.
J. N. Banerjea, *The Development of Hindu Iconography* (1956), Pl. 17.1.

Dark-green, indurated talc.* Nose chipped; right arm with lance and head of cock broken; upper right corner chipped 1′ 10 3/16″ x 11 5/8″

33. KHASARPAṆA LOKEŚVARA

Chauduar, Orissa, twelfth century.

(PLATES 12–13)

The Bodhisattva Avalokiteśvara in his form as Khasarpaṇa is seated in "graceful posture" (lalitāsana) with the left leg rested on the double lotus throne, the right leg pendant and supported by a small double lotus in the pedestal. His body is flexed in a slight curve; the right hand rests on the knee in the boon-giving (varada) gesture. Below it, in the pedestal (13) is the small figure of demon Sūcīmukha ("needle mouth"). He looks up adoringly to the Bodhisattva waiting for the drop of honey which he will be able to swallow from the stream of nectar that flows from the hand of Khasarpaṇa. The left hand of the god, which is raised, holds the stalk of the lotus. The crown of the Bodhisattva is piled with matted locks. The ornaments are similar to those of Kārttikeya (10) but for the necklace and the sacred thread over the left shoulder. These ornaments have a fringe of pearl tassels; the hip-belt and anklets are set with bells. Streamers flutter upward, right and left, of the crown.

The slab is carved like the back of a throne (p. 88). Its posts show the symbols of the lion (vyālaka) rearing over a prostrate and small elephant. Strings of pearls issue from the lion's mouth. The posts support an elaborate crossbar. From it springs a jewel-studded trefoil arch. The slab is cut between the figure of the god and the frame of the throne. On the crossbar are Kinnaras, here shown as bird-legged gnomes, their hair bristling around their heads. One plays the lute (vīṇā); the other holds a flower (?). On top, Vidyādharas (holders of knowledge) are flying; the one on the left playing on the ḍamaru (drum); the other holding a flower (?). A "face of glory" (kīrttimukha) in the centre exhales scrolls of vapour. These, as well as the symbols of the throne, are a recurrent setting for divinities. The four deities associated with Khasarpaṇa squat on either side of the lotus throne and the pedestal.

Next to the boon-giving hand of Khasarpaṇa is the small figure of Sudhanakumāra wearing a high, conical cap; he has the appearance of a prince and carries a book under his arm. His hands are folded in worship. Behind the left knee of the god is Hayagrīva, a squat, demoniac personage.

The goddesses are shown in the pedestal; to the right of the god is Tārā. Her right hand, with the gesture of exposition, touches and her left hand holds an opening lotus bud. There are flowers in her chignon. Her face is suffused with loving tenderness (13). On the opposite edge of the pedestal, Bhṛkuṭī, who wears a crown of matted locks, raises one hand in adoration (vandana) and carries a staff (tridaṇḍin), water vessel, and rosary in her three other hands. Between the foot of Khasarpaṇa and Bhṛkuṭī a pillar rises above an altar and supports a diminutive lotus and on it the light-giving, wish-granting, flamelike "Jewel." To either side, within the convoluted "lotus" tendrils, are the other six "treasures" which come into existence when a Cakravartin, a universal ruler, of the outer or of the inner world, is born. They are wheel, elephant, horse, queen, minister, and general—a sword is substituted for the general. Their small shapes occupy the plane

* Dr. Paul J. Storm, Department of Earth Sciences, University of Pennsylvania, examined the stones of the sculptures.

behind the kneeling figures of the woman-donor and her child.

The differences in scale of the figures—in this and other images—are dictated by the relative importance of the figures in their context. Here they are dominated by the shape of Khasarpaṇa. "His glance is moist with compassion. He breathes love."

41.23.1

Brown indurated talc. Left arm broken; face and right hand damaged 2′ 7¾″ x 1′ 3⅞″

34. MITHUNA *Bhuvaneshvar, Orissa, late eleventh century.*

(PLATE 14)

With its large, unadorned planes, this small sculpture, carved nearly in the round, yields clear-cut silhouettes.

Both the figures wear large chignons at the backs of their heads. The bracelet is of the same type as in (7) but omits details. The large ear ornaments of the man and the woman are part of the sculptural form. The sculpture resembles some of the carvings of the Brahmeśvar temple which is inscribed in the year 1073 (R. C. Mazumdar, *A History of the Indian People,* "The Struggle for Empire," V, 211).

56.75.17

Published: *Journal of the Indian Society of Oriental Art,* II (1934), Pl. XX.
Buff sandstone. Traces of red pigmentation; nose of female figure chipped, broken at chest; male figure broken at thigh, his right hand broken 1′ 2¼″ x 7 5/16″

35. BOAR, FOLIAGE, AND SCROLLS *Koṇārak, Orissa, 1238–64.*

(PLATE 15)

Fragment from lower part of wall (or of wheel carved on the wall). Cf. *The Art of Indian Asia,* Pls. 359, 360. The modelled shape of the boar, the deeply undercut scrolls with their oblique planes are harmonized in a rich and dramatic play of light and shade.

56.75.9

Buff sandstone. Slightly weathered 2⅝″ x 4½″

36. DUEL CĀRAṆĪ *Koṇārak, Orissa, 1238–64.*

(PLATE 16)

The sculpture of this genie was placed on top of a temple tower, the Śikhara, and below its crowning member (āmalaka). Four such figures, in the four directions, supported the āmalaka. The Cāraṇas are "movers at will" and guard the temple. Their images show them squatting, pressing down the lofty building while the corrugated rim of the āmalaka rests on their broad heads. (Cf. *The Hindu Temple,* p. 356.) The compact volume of the squatter, comprising locks and face, expresses the function and position of the Deul Cāraṇī on the monument. Its place is above the—generally—figureless trunk of the superstructure (p. 45).

56.75.40

Published: *Journal of the Indian Society of Oriental Art,* II (1934), Pl. XXIII, Fig. 1.
Sandstone. Blackened, weathered; left part of base broken 11½″ x 8½″

37. MITHUNA *Find-place unknown, Orissa, thirteenth century.*

(PLATES 17–18)

The naked figures—almost carved in the round—wear few ornaments, amongst which those above the anklets are noteworthy. (Cf. *The Art of Indian Asia,* Pl. 362.)

56.75.18

Black indurated talc. Right foot of male figure broken; hair slightly chipped 10¾″ x 7⅝″

38. MITHUNA *Bhuvaneshvar, Orissa, thirteenth century.*

Supported by a console with architectural mouldings topped by a lotus, the hero (vīra) places the right foot on a tree stump (?) and turns towards his consort who leans against his chest. The lively movement of the group is extended to the branches of a tree above the high coiffures of the figures.

56.75.16

Buff sandstone. Traces of red pigment in pedestal; mortise in upper edge of slab; upper part battered 1′ 10″ x 6″

39. GAJA-SIṂHA *Find-place unknown, Orissa, twelfth to thirteenth century.*

(PLATE 58)[1]

The elephant-headed, lion-bodied shape of the Gaja-Siṃha rears above a rugged mountain inhabited by diminutive animal shapes. It has seized in its trunk and forepaws a demoniacal figure holding dagger and shield. The group is in the round and follows the curve of the ivory tusk out of which it was carved. A circular socle and a quadrangular headpiece indicate the function of the sculpture. Apparently it was one of the legs of a throne. If the front corner of the square headpiece corresponds to a corner of the seat, the inward curve of the sculpture reduces the width of the base of the throne. Ivory throne legs of later date use the curve of the tusk in the opposite direction. This increases the area of support.

The subject of the Gaja-Siṃha with the demon dangling in its grip is familiar from stone sculptures in Koṇārak. The style of the carving points in the same direction although it is even more closely related to that of Plate 12, where the faces of the Kinnaras, their hair and ornaments, agree with those of the demon on the ivory. The firmness of the modelling and precision of detail are of the same degree in these two sculptures. The livelier style of the image of Khasarpaṇa precedes the formalised generalisations, the tightened contour, and meticulous wealth of jewelry of the Sūrya images of Koṇārak.

60.96.1

Gift of Mrs. John B. Stetson
Published in the *Philadelphia Museum Bulletin,* LIV (Spring 1959), 55–66.
J. E. van Lohuizen-de Leeuw, "Indian Ivories with special reference to a Mediaeval Throne Leg from Orissa," *Arts Asiatiques,* XX (1960), 13–21.
Ivory. Socket in top of carving; base cut; ears broken; left claw of left hindleg restored; mountain crags and one claw of each foreleg chipped; bracelets rubbed; discolored, dark spots due to fabric in which the sculpture was wrapped 13½″ x 5⅛″ x 5⅛″

[1] The carving was given to the Museum when the catalogue was already in print. The plate illustrating the Gaja-Siṃha could not be included among those from Orissa.

BIHĀR-BENGAL (PĀLA AND SENA DYNASTIES)

40. BUDDHA SUBDUES THE RAGING ELEPHANT NĀLAGIRI *Bodh-gayā, Bihār, second half ninth century.*

A raging elephant was let loose by Devadatta, the Buddha's jealous cousin, so that it should kill the Buddha, when as a monk he went begging for his food in the streets of Rājagṛha. The Buddha met the raging animal with kindness, and the elephant bowed before the Buddha.

The relief slab, rounded on top, is filled by the walking figure of the Buddha. He stands on a double lotus on his right leg; the left is bent in the knee; the feet are turned to the right. The right hand is lowered towards the elephant whose diminutive shape occupies the extreme right of the slab. From the right hand of the Buddha issue miniature "lions"—indicative of his lion-power (p. 83). The raised left hand holds the end of his robe (saṅghāṭī). This is shown transparent and covers both shoulders down to the hands. Its hem, raised in relief, forms a rectangular outline whose one side passes over the legs. Below and parallel to it is the hem of the undergarment (antaravāsaka). A deep line across the hips indicates where this garment is fastened tightly around the body. The nimbate head is flanked by two miniature stūpas.

On the extreme right stands a monk carrying bowl and staff. A double torus moulding surrounds the back of the slab. The same device outlines the halo. The base of the slab, with its central projection (triratha), is inscribed with the formula of the Buddhist creed (p. 83).

Cf. R. D. Banerji, "The Eastern Indian School of Mediaeval Sculpture," *Archaeological Survey of India, New Imperial Series,* XLVII (Delhi, 1933), Pls. II, IIIc. Stella Kramrisch, "Pāla and Sena Sculpture," *Rūpaṃ* (1929), opp. p. 110, description of Fig. 10.

21.36.15

Basalt. Base broken on left; slab chipped on top 1′ 1⅜″ x 8⅜″

41. BUDDHA SUBDUES THE RAGING ELEPHANT NĀLAGIRI *Find-place unknown, Bihār, second half ninth century.*

(PLATE 19)

In the two images (21.36.15; 56.75.49), the Buddha is shown as a monk. In this shape he had been known to his disciples. In this shape he reveals himself to man (Nirmāṇakāya). The shape in which he reveals himself to the elect, the Bodhisattvas, is his Sambhogakāya, the glorious body of conjoined beatitude. This body wears jewels above the monk's robe and is crowned. (P. Mus, "Le Bouddha Paré," *Bulletin de l'Ecole Française d'Extrême Orient,* XXVIII [1928], 194.) The lowered right is held palm inward and is surrounded by the plain surface of a block, indicative of the Buddha's webbed fingers. The elephant bows reverentially and is even smaller than in the other image (21.36.15).

The bead-edged slab of the relief which was part of an architectural setting is flanked by circular, baluster-shaped pillars in pot bases. From the crossbar above their capitals springs a trefoil arch, the extrados accompanied by Kinnara and Kinnarī musicians ensconced in a wave and scroll design.

56.75.49

Basalt. Slightly damaged 1′ 11⅛″ x 11$^{13}/_{16}$″

42. BUDDHA CALLING THE EARTH TO WITNESS *Bihār, ca. 900.*

When Māra, the Evil one, assaulted Siddhārtha, the Bodhisattva called the earth to witness, that on account of his charity he was entitled to be seated on the throne of the world.

The Buddha, seated cross-legged on a double lotus, with right arm pendant over right leg, touches the lotus with the finger tips, the left leg resting in "dhyāna-mudrā" on the right foot. The Saṅghātī covers the left shoulder. A betel leaf-shaped, flame-edged halo (śiraścakra) surrounding the head rises from the crossbar of the throne supporting the lotus. The pañcaratha pedestal is covered by a draped cloth in the middle, flanked by a four-petalled lotus flower on the adjacent ratha. Baluster-shaped pillars with folded cloth streamer attached. Large bolster behind back of Buddha. Two stūpas above the crossbar flank the nimbate head, surmounted by a triple device of bodhi tree leaves. Inscribed on back of slab with the Buddhist creed formula: *Ye dharmmā hetuprabhavā hetuṃ teṣām Tathāgato hy avadat teṣām ca yo nirodha evaṃvādī mahāsramaṇah.* ("The states of being which arise from a basis—their basis the Tathāgata has told and their cessation—this the great monk tells.")

21.36.12

Basalt. Nose and right hand slightly damaged 7½" x 6⅛"

43. BUDDHA CALLING THE EARTH TO WITNESS *Bodh-gayā, Bihār, tenth century.*

The Buddha is seated cross-legged (vajraparyaṅka) on a double lotus on a lion throne. The lotus is a symbol of total manifestation, the support of existence and matrix of divinity. The lion throne is the seat of power. All power being derived from the sun, the lion is the symbol of that power. A cloth is draped over the throne. The cloak of the Buddha covers the left shoulder. The rounded slab is edged with flames. It represents the prabhāmaṇḍala, the Buddha's effulgence.

21.36.16

Basalt. Traces of gilding on image 9" x 6¼"

44. BUDDHA CALLING THE EARTH TO WITNESS *Bengal, late eleventh-twelfth century.*

Lower part of image only. Of the scenes surrounding the figure of Buddha, which were carved on the back of the slab, the Birth (Figure of Māyā?) on the right and the offering of the monkey on the left are partly preserved.

The "double lotus" throne (mahāṃbujapīṭha) has a saptaratha pedestal, with the figure of Bhū-devī in the centre, the donor on the right, Māra and a demon on the left. On the extreme left are two fire-bowls (agni kuṇḍa). Inscription on pedestal written inverted as mirror picture (?).

31.60.11

Gift of N. M. Heeramaneck
Black talc-schist. 8$^{11}/_{16}$" x 9$^{7}/_{16}$"

45. CROWNED BUDDHA PREACHING *Bodh-gayā, Bihār, eleventh century.*
(PLATE 20)

The Buddha, seated in the "adamantine," unshakeable posture (vajraparyaṅka), holds the hands in front of his chest in the gesture of preaching (*dharma-cakra pravar ttana* ["turning the wheel of the law."]). To the right and left of him are smaller images of the Buddha in monk's robe. They represent, the one on the right with boon-giving gesture (varada mudrā), the episode of the raging elephant; the one on the left, with his hand raised in the gesture of fearlessness (abhaya mudrā), a similar episode, where assassins employed by Devadatta were subdued by the Buddha.

To either side of the head of the Buddha a seated image of the Buddha on a lotus has the hands on the lap in the gesture of meditation (dhyāna mudrā) holding a bowl of honey which a monkey had offered to the Buddha.

The small flower canopy on top indicates the grove at Sārnāth where the Buddha preached his first sermon.

Triratha base incomplete.

21.36.13

Basalt. Hands battered; right corner of base broken 9⅞″ x 8⅙″

46. CROWNED BUDDHA, WITH OFFERING OF THE MONKEY *Bodh-gayā, Bihār, eleventh century.*

The image is surrounded by the following scenes: the birth of the Buddha, the subduing of the elephant, the calling of the earth to witness, and the Great Decease (parinirvāṇa) on top, the first sermon, the subduing of the assassins, the miracle at Śrāvastī. Two miniature stūpas are on either side above the Buddha's halo, which is surmounted by an umbrella; at the top of the slab, spirit hands coming out of clouds beat a drum and clash cymbals.

21.36.14

Basalt. Hands and pedestal damaged 11½″ x 7¼″

47. MAÑJUVARA(?) *Find-place unknown, Bihār, ca. twelfth century.*

The Bodhisattva is seated in vajraparyaṅka on a lotus. The hands are held in front of the chest. Locks fall over the shoulders. The image wears rich jewelry.

A Vajra or thunderbolt is carved on the cloth placed over the throne as a symbol of its "adamantine" (vajra), unshakeable quality.

31.60.6

Gift of N. M. Heeramaneck
Basalt. Top and sides broken; hands damaged; battered 9½″ x 6⅞″

48. MINIATURE VOTIVE SHRINE *Bodh-gayā, Bihār, tenth century.*

The trefoil niche on the face of the shrine surrounds the image of Buddha calling the earth to witness; in the smaller niches on the other three sides are: Buddha preaching, on right proper of main niche; on the left, Bodhisattva Mañjuśrī; and at the back, Bodhisattva Avalokiteśvara. The arch of the niches is surrounded by lotus and scrollwork. The spire of the Triratha shrine is a slightly curvilinear Śikhara. It shows in the middle of each side a sequence of Gavākṣas. They are flanked by corner sequences of two Gavākṣas with an āmalaka between them. The square top platform (vedi) and neck (grīvā) are broad. The āmalaka is surmounted by two series of mouldings of diminishing diameter.

Two short inscriptions on two faces of the base read: *Guṇakāra Kīrtī* ("the glory of Guṇakāra") and *Śa*[?] *śidevadharmoyaṃ* ("the religious gift of Śaśideva").

21.36.7

Basalt. 1′ 8$\frac{5}{16}$″ x 7$\frac{3}{16}$″

49. VOTIVE STŪPA *Bodh-gayā, Bihār, tenth century.*

Above a high square base and architectural mouldings the stūpa shows within a niche the Buddha "calling the earth to witness." The stūpa is surmounted by a square harmikā and platformlike slab above which rises a cone of four "umbrellas" (chattravallī) surmounted by a bud-shaped finial. The base is inscribed in two lines with the formula of the Buddhist creed. (Cf. 21.36.12.)

The third line of the inscription is not wholly legible.

21.36.11

Basalt. 9″ x 4″

50. VOTIVE STŪPA *Bihār, ca. 900.*

The four niches show 1) the Buddha preaching, 2) calling the earth to witness, 3) holding the offering of the monkey, and 4) calling the earth to witness. The niches are capped by pyramidal Śikharas with āmalakas. Above them are two torus mouldings and a "double lotus."

21.36.9

Basalt. 1′ 4½″ x 1′ 2$^{3}/_{16}$″

51. VOTIVE STŪPA *Bihār, ca. 900.*

Cf. 21.36.9.

21.36.10

1′ 4″ x 1′ 1½″

52. FACING OF STŪPA BASE *Bihār, eleventh century.*

Buddha preaching, surrounded by niche. Above this, in a smaller niche, is an image of Buddha calling the earth to witness.

The mouldings, overlapped by, and on either side of, the niches, are divided by a deep recess—cyma and torus carved in low relief with a railing pattern.

21.36.3

Basalt. 1′ 1$^{5}/_{16}$″ x 1′ $^{3}/_{16}$″

53. FACING OF STŪPA BASE *Bihār, eleventh century.*

From the same monument as 21.36.3. In the upper niche the Buddha is seated in meditation, the hands in dhyāna mudrā.

21.36.4

Basalt. 1′ 1⅝″ x 1′

54. NICHE FOR IMAGE *Bodh-gayā, Bihār, tenth century.*

The pillars of the trefoil niche rise from pot bases. Above their bracket capitals, Haṃsa birds with their plumage surround the arch and lead to the "Jewel in the Lotus" at its apex. The carving of the niche overlaps architectural mouldings with Gavākṣa devices. The architectural moulding above the niche is overlapped by three niches, surrounding two standing Buddha images representing the raging elephant and the assassin episodes and a Buddha seated with dhyāna mudrā.

21.36.1

Basalt. Interior of niche chiselled away 1′ 8$^{5}/_{16}$″ x 1′ ⅜″

55. CORNER STONE *Bodh-gayā, Bihār, tenth century.*

In three trefoil niches with baluster-shaped pillars are seated Buddha images, one in earth-touching attitude in the middle, the two others in meditation. On the adjacent face of the stone is an image in earth-touching attitude within the same kind of niche. The spandrels are filled with triangular "lotus with jewel" devices.

21.36.2

Basalt. 7⅝" x 1′ 5⁵⁄₁₆"

56. ARCHITECTURAL FRAGMENT *Bodh-gayā, Bihār, eleventh century.*

The Buddha images in the four niches are seated in meditation (1–3), the fourth in earth-touching attitude. Half lotuses in spandrels of niches.

21.36.6

Basalt. 4⁷⁄₁₆" x 1′ 3⅝"

57. ARCHITECTURAL FRAGMENT *Bodh-gayā, Bihār, late tenth century.*

In four trefoil niches with baluster-shaped pillars, three of the standing Buddha images show the gesture of "giving a boon"; the second, but last, image shows the gesture of fearlessness, a flamelike device in the spandrels.

21.36.5

Basalt. 6⅜" x 1′ 4¾"

58. VOTIVE TABLET *Find-place unknown, Bihār, eleventh century.*

Buddha calling the earth to witness is seated on lotus above triratha altar in trefoil niche supported by columns with pot capitals. The extrados of the trefoil arc are set with āmalakas. The trefoil niche is surmounted by a pyramidal śikhara of three rathas. Above its platform (vedi) the long neck (grīvā), supports an āmalaka with a stūpa-like finial. Miniature stūpas, streamers, and leaves fill the tablet within its beaded outline. It is surrounded by a thick, raised rim.
Inscribed with the Buddhist creed.

21.36.18

Terracotta. Left elbow damaged 6¹⁵⁄₁₆" x 4⁹⁄₁₆"

59. VOTIVE TABLET

Duplicate of 21.36.18.

21.36.19

Rim battered on left

60. NĀGARĀJA AND QUEEN *Find-place unknown, Bihār, tenth century.*

(PLATE 21)

The Mithuna of the serpent king and queen is surmounted by the fan-shaped canopy of their serpent hoods and ends with their interlacing serpent bodies. The king, with his right arm around the queen, holds a garland against her shoulder. His left lowered hand rests on his thigh and holds the other end of the garland so that the curve of the garland passes over the bodies of the Nāgarāja and his queen, where they change from human into serpent shape. The right arm of the serpent queen is held up in kaṭaka hasta against the chest of the king; her left rests on his left shoulder. He wears a tiered crown (karaṇḍa mukuṭa). The queen wears a crested diadem in front of her broad, flat chignon. Festoons of pearls are attached to their hip-belts. The fivefold hood of the king and the triple hood of the queen are marked with wave lines indicating the rippling serpent bodies. Below the head of each serpent a large trefoil symbol is raised and outlined in low relief.

This symbol is carved all over the cloak of the priestly figure from Mohenjo-daro, of the later part of the third millennium B.C. (*The Art of Indian Asia,* Pl. 1.) The same symbol is repeated on a railing pillar from Mathurā (L. Ashton [ed.], *The Art of India and Pakistan,* Pl. 8, Fig. 53), below the figure of a girl bathing under a waterfall. It appears that this trefoil is a symbol of the waters.

The Nāga Kingdom is in the Waters. Its capital city is Bhogavatī, the town of enjoyment. The nature of the Nāgas is passionate. Their intertwining tails form a serpent coil (nāgapāśa) which is also a love-knot (premapāśa).

The back of the sculpture formed by the serpent-foil is flat and has a large tenon in the middle by which the sculpture was fixed to a building.

56.75.45

Published: *The Art of India and Pakistan,* Pl. 41, Fig. 273.
Philadelphia Museum Bulletin, LII (1957), 35.
Cf. *The Eastern Indian School of Mediaeval Sculpture,* Pl. LXV, a and c.
Gabbro. Top chipped; noses battered 3′ 5 7/16″ x 1′ 4 1/4″

61. VIṢṆU ON GARUḌA *Bodh-gayā, Bihār, tenth century.*

Viṣṇu seated on the winged arms of squatting, pot-bellied Garuḍa, his mount, holds a club in the right and a conch in the left of his raised upper hands. The two main hands are joined in front of the chest. Two goddesses with fly whisks in their right hands are seated in postures of ease, the pendant legs supported on a lotus flower, on either side of the god. A cushion seat supports the group. The broad slab is arched.

21.36.17

Basalt. Left edge of slab and figure on left broken; noses battered 5 13/16″ x 7 7/16″

62. CAṆḌĪ *Find-place unknown, North Bengal, eleventh century.*

(PLATES 22–23)

The goddess stands stiffly and firmly on her feet (samapādasthānaka) on a double lotus base above a triply projected (pañcaratha) pedestal. Her four hands hold: a Śiva liṅga (?) in the upper right, a pomegranate in the lower right in front of a lotus support, her lower left rests on the head of Kārttikeya, the upper left holds a mirror. The goddess wears a crown of matted locks; long ribbons flutter from her crown.

A pointed nimbus of two mouldings rises from the shoulders to the lotus-crested crown (23). The betel leaf-shaped face of Caṇḍī, "the Wrathful," has a vertical mark across the forehead indicating the third eye. The flutter of lids and brow with their double curves plays over the set face of the goddess (23). The richly bejewelled figure wears a long skirt, and a scarf passes from her left shoulder across her breasts. To her right stands Gaṇeśa holding a battle axe (paraśu) in his lowered right. The trunk of his elephant head is bent to the left where it takes up the ball of sweetmeat held in the left hand. To the left of the goddess stands Kārttikeya in tribhaṅga. Flowing garments accompany his stance. Behind the two small figures are banana plants on the extreme right and left of this cult image.

In the pedestal the straight stalk of the lotus in the middle issues from a double lotus and continues the vertical of the goddess. To the right, on the second step (ratha) is an alligator (godhā), an animal associated with the Great Goddess; to the left, on the second ratha is a kneeling worshipper, the donor.

The pedestal supports the three divinities, each stationed on a double lotus. The back of the slab behind them suggests the back of a throne. It ends with a pointed arch and is cut out around the figure of Caṇḍī. The back of the throne shows the full sequence of symbols: the leogryph (śārdūla)—vomiting pearls—above the elephant; the Makara at the height of the crossbar; on the crossbar the Kinnara-musicians, their bodies ending in a trail of feathery scrolls; above these, where the arch springs, are flying Vidyādharas, with their offerings in front of foaming clouds. At the top is the pointed "face of glory" from whose open mouth escape two Makaras. The configuration of the symbols on the back of the throne shows, symbolically, the threefold structure of the cosmos (cf. J. Auboyer, *Le Trône et Son Symbolism dans L'Inde Ancienne* [Paris, 1949], p. 134). The elephant is the support of the world and symbolizes in this configuration the solid earth. The leogryph or "lion" (p. 83) symbolizes the solar power of manifestation. Above this configuration is the head of the Makara, the elephant-headed great monster of the waters. In Indian astrology the Makara denotes the place of Capricorn. It symbolises the arising from Darkness into the light world. The light world is that of the celestial sphere where the symbols of the heavenly ocean of light and vapours are, above the level of the Makaras of the crossbar. This part of the throne begins above the shoulders of the goddess.

56.75.15

Black talc-schist. Slightly weathered; tip of nose broken; liṅga damaged; top broken 1′ 8¾″ x 10⅛″

63. SŪRYA *Gaṅgā Sāgarī, Saugor Island, Bengal, late twelfth century.*

(PLATES 24–25)

Sūrya, the Sun god, is shown driving forward on his chariot of seven horses. The horses are allotted to the seven steps of the (saptaratha) pedestal. A circle around the central horse indicates the one and only wheel of the Sun god's chariot, which is the cycle of the year. Above the pedestal arises the Sun god, standing straight in samapādasthānaka on a double lotus pedestal. His two hands raised to the chest hold each a lotus flower at the level of his face. In front of the Sun god is the small image of his wife Uṣas (25), the Dawn of the World. In her right hand she holds a rosary against her chest; her pendant left holds a water vessel. In the foremost plane of the relief, in front of Uṣas on her lotus pedestal, Aruṇa, the Sun god's leg-less charioteer, wields the reins above the head of a Makara. To either side of Aruṇa, in the lowest plane of the relief —flanking the booted legs of the Sun god—are his two other wives, Sureṇu (Saraṇyu), the daughter of heaven, and Chāyā, her shadow, whose name is also Pṛithivī, the earth. Both hold fly whisks in their right hands. On the second step of the pedestal are two diminutive female archers, the two dawns of morning and evening (Uṣā and Pratyuṣā). Behind them, to the right of Sūrya, on the first step of the chariot and standing on a double lotus base of his own, is the large figure of heavy-limbed, bearded Piṅgala, the recorder of the Sun god, carrying ink pot and pen. Youthful

Daṇḍa, Sūrya's measurer, stands on the left. He carries sword and shield, decorated with the sun and crescent moon. Behind and above these gods and carved as diminutive figures are the planets, including those of the "eclipse-demons"—on the right of Sūrya from above downward—Bṛhaspati (Jupiter) with book and rosary; Śani (Saturn) with bow and arrow; Maṅgala (Mars) holding a spear; and Soma, the moon, holding a water pot. On the left of Sūrya from below upwards: Śukra (Venus) with rosary and water pot; Budha (Mercury) with a mace and boon-giving gesture; Rāhu, the eclipse-demon whose two hands hold the unobscured part of the luminary's disc; and Ketu, whose body ends with a serpent tail, holding sword and flame (?).

Above the planets (graha) are Vidyādharas carrying garlands in their hands, and their music-playing wives on their legs. The point of the slab is occupied by a Face of Glory from whose jaw issue chubby celestials (gaṇa) wielding a dagger, in front of clouds.

The slab is bordered by scrolls and has an inner scroll border on top, between the Vidyādharas. There the innermost part of the relief ground is carved in the likeness of flames, on either side of Sūrya's crown. This high, conical crown ends with two āmalakas. The Sun god wears a short bodice covering chest and arms. The hem of the bodice is indented. A dagger stuck into his loincloth behind the particularly broad hip-belt and a sword attached to his long garland are the weapons of this highly ornate image of Sūrya. The fluttering ends of the scarf next to his hands and those of the bands of the crown are as formalised as are the cusped eyebrows. The eyes dilated in divine fury (krodha) have the pupils marked with lotuses. A vertical line traverses the forehead.

27.9.1

Gift of Mrs. N. R. Norton, Mrs. Richard Waln Meirs, Mrs. Edwin N. Benson, Jr., Mrs. William A. M. Fuller in memory of Sabine W. Wister

Cf. *Bulletin of the Pennsylvania Museum* No. 20 (October, 1907), p. 68.

Black talc-schist. Noses slightly damaged 5′ 5″ x 2′ 7¼″

64. KṚṢṆA *Bengal, ca. fifteenth century.*

Standing with left hip thrown out. Hair gathered on top of head in a high cone clasped by a ring at base. The statuette is carved in the round.

31.60.5

Gift of N. M. Heeramaneck

Grey-black schist. Arms and lower parts of legs missing; face weathered 9¾″ x 3¼″

SCULPTURES FROM THE GANGES-YAMUNĀ REGION (VĀRĀṆASĪ TO MATHURĀ) UTTAR PRADESH

(related to Candella School, p. 91)

65. DANCING GAṆA *Vārāṇasī, eleventh century.*

(PLATE 26)

The chubby figure with both knees bent (caturasra) stands flexed in all the joints (atibhaṅga) on the left foot and touches the ground with the toes of the right foot. The right hand was raised to the shoulder; the left carried a staff(?). The hair, dressed in corkscrew curls, falls to the shoulders; the ears are elongated. Only the body wears jewelry.

56.75.43

Buff sandstone. Arms and crown of head damaged; weathered 1′ 10¼″ x 10³⁄₁₆″

66. UMĀ-MAHEŚVARA *Vicinity of Allahabad, tenth to eleventh century.*

Images of this type show Śiva, the Great Lord, lovingly together with his power in the form of the goddess (Umā). Śiva is enthroned (lalitāsana) on a high seat; his pendant right leg rests on a cushion. Umā, seated on his left leg, has her left leg drawn up resting her foot on the god's knee; her pendant right leg rests (sukhāsana) on her mount, the lion. Śiva holds in his upper right his serpent-entwined trident; his lower right caresses the chin of the goddess (the fingers are unusually lengthened); his upper left holds a deer(?) above the head of Umā. His lower left is cupped under her breast. The goddess rests her right hand on Śiva's right shoulder. In the left, she holds a curved metal mirror. The richly bejewelled figures wear each a short loincloth. A scarf is draped round Śiva's right leg.

To the right of Śiva is his devotee Bhṛṅgī, his hair dressed in jatābhara. He carries a cup and a pronged staff. In front of him is Gaṇeśa. Kārttikeya on his peacock is below the lion's mouth. Nandin, Śiva's mount, is shown in the middle with his head raised towards Śiva's foot. The squatting figure between Nandin and Kārttikeya is defaced. Jayā and Vijayā, the maids in attendance, kneel at the corners of the throne. A standing figure left of Umā (Nārada?) wearing jaṭāmukuṭa and carrying a staff(?) balances the standing figure of Bhṛṅgī on the other side. Above these two figures are the rampant lions (śārdūla) which form part of the throne (p. 88). On the crossbar above them are large Makara heads, on either side of the halo whose wide arc surmounts the heads of the god and goddess while its sunk circular centre is behind Śiva's high crown of matted hair.

The proportions of the back of the throne allow the images to occupy the region below the crossbar and the Makara. Śiva as Umā-Maheśvara is envisaged in manifestation. His transcendental nature has its symbol in the five Liṅgas (cf. the five faces of Śiva, p. 98) on a lotus base, above the nimbus, in the middle of the slightly rounded top of the slab.

56.75.47

Buff sandstone. Weathered; object in upper left of Śiva defaced; legs damaged 1′ 7¾″ x 1′ ⁵⁄₁₆″

67. HEAD OF ŚIVA *Vicinity of Allahabad, tenth to eleventh century.*

(PLATE 28)

The high crown of braided hair is tied with a scarf crossing in the middle above the festooned diadem. This is worn high on the head and allows the pure outline of the hair to demarcate the wide forehead.

56.75.48

Buff sandstone. Top damaged, slightly battered 9⁷⁄₁₆″ x 4½″

68. TWO DISCIPLES IN CONVERSATION *Vicinity of Allahabad, eleventh century.*

(PLATE 27)

The seated figures of the boys, facing one another in three-quarter profile, are naked. Their hair is tied in a mango-shaped bun at the back of the head. The telling gestures of their right hands are set off by the left hand of the larger boy resting on the ground and that of the smaller boy resting on his knee and holding a fruit(?). The rooflet of the rectangular niche is supported by square pilasters and has a gavākṣa in the centre.

56.75.46

Buff sandstone. Base and top damaged 10¼″ x 1′ 1⁵⁄₁₆″

69. APSARAS *Vicinity of Allahabad, tenth century.*

The celestial raises her right arm along the back of the head with its small bun. The forearm vaults over the head and touches the hair ornament, in front. A long, double pearl chain hangs from the necklace to the loincloth which is held by a hip zone (mekhalā). The folds of the end of the cloth hang over the mekhalā. The body in its torsion is masterfully modelled.

56.75.4

Buff sandstone. Weathered 11⅝″ x 5½″

70. NIRṚITI(?) or KṢETRAPĀLA *Vicinity of Aligarh, Uttar Pradesh, eleventh century.*

The young, male, naked figure stands with a slight bend (ābhaṅga) in front of a prostrate small figure. In its right hand the standing figure holds a sword, pointing upwards, and with the left it clutches the long hair of a decapitated head. The hair of the image stands up above a diadem in the conventional design indicating horripilation. A large, plain nimbus rises from behind the shoulders.

The image stands on a console, under a "baldachin" moulding. A large leaf shape is carved below it on either side on the edge of the pier.

Nirṛiti is the guardian and Lord of the southwestern region. Although the image does not correspond to a known formula of visualisation (dhyāna) for Nirṛiti, related types occur on extant temples (Dūlādeo, Khajurāho).

56.75.6

Grey dolomitic limestone. Socle damaged, nose battered 3′ 3¹⁄₁₆″ x 1′ ¹⁄₁₆″

CENTRAL INDIA

71. VIDYĀDHARA *Find-place unknown, central India, ca. eighth century.*

The Vidyādhara carries a garland and flies in front of a cloud, his left leg thrown backward, the foot touching his head.

31.60.13

Gift of N. M. Heeramaneck
Dark reddish buff sandstone. Weathered, battered 7″ x 9″

a) *Candella School (Northern Central India)*

72. UMĀ-MAHEŚVARA *Khajurāho, eleventh century.*

(PLATE 29)

Cf. 56.75.47 (66).

The right hands of Śiva show a trident, varada mudrā; the lower left touches Pārvatī's breast, the upper left holds a three-hooded serpent. The pendant legs of the divinities rest each on a lotus. A lotus is incised on the front of the pañcaratha pedestal. The back of the throne has Makara heads on the crossbar above posts with wave design, a small attendant on each side, in front of the post. Above the right proper and left of the nimbus of Śiva are the standing figures of Brahmā and Gaṇeśa respectively. Above the jaṭāmukuṭa of Śiva and supported on a lotus-podlike salver are eight Liṅgas, symbolic of the eight aspects of Śiva (aṣṭamūrti). The level where the Liṅgas are carved is marked by a second crossbar on either side of the lotus pod.

56.75.28

Cream sandstone. Weathered, slightly battered; one corner of pedestal chipped 1′ ⅞″ x 7½″

73. GAṆEŚA AND ŚAKTI *Khajurāho, tenth century.*

(PLATE 30)

The elephant-headed, serpent-entwined god holds in his upper right hand the axe (paraśu), and in his upper left a serpent-entwined bowl heaped with balls of sweetmeat (laḍḍu). His lower left rests on the waist of the Śakti. In a gesture of love, the elephant trunk is turned towards the left foot of the Śakti, which rests on her right thigh.

The figures are seated on a cushion seat, over which fall the folds of Gaṇeśa's lower garment. The lobes of his forehead are wreathed with jewel chains pendant from a Face of Glory that crowns his head. Although Gaṇeśa has only one tusk, by sculptural convention both the tusks are shown (the left as a stump; the other as a full-sized tusk). The goddess wears her hair in tiers in the shape of a karaṇḍamukuṭa. Ringed columns flank the image.

56.75.22

Published: A. Getty, *Gaṇeśa,* Pl. 4a.
Cream sandstone. Top and right lower hand of Gaṇeśa broken; right tusk chipped; slightly battered 1′ 8$\frac{1}{16}$″ x 1′ 4$\frac{11}{16}$″

74. HEAD OF ŚIVA *Khajurāho, tenth century.*

The head is crowned with a jaṭāmukuṭā.

56.75.31

Buff sandstone. Top broken; battered 7⅝″ x 5$\frac{1}{16}$″

75. KUBERA *Khajurāho, tenth to eleventh century.*

(PLATE 32)

Kubera, King of Yakṣas, Lord of treasures hidden in the earth, and Guardian of the northern quarter, is shown heavy-bodied, seated with right leg pendant, the right hand holding a club (gadā) to which the blade of a battle axe (paraśu) is attached. The left holds on a serpentlike leash a mongoose vomiting jewels. God and animal wear pearl strings. The serpentlike leash is slung over the left shoulder of Kubera. His hair is dressed standing up in horripilation (cf. 70), for, though the Kubera here shows no fangs, his cruel nature is thus shown.

A ringed column to the right proper and a canopy of several mouldings—some carved behind a Gavākṣa pediment—form the architectural setting of this image.

Inscription on base; *Ṣajuḥ* (the name of the craftsman).

56.75.26

Cream sandstone. Top battered 1′ 7¾″ x 7⅜″

76. DEVĪ *Khajurāho, tenth century.*

(PLATE 36)

The hands of the goddess are folded between her breasts. An attendant goddess on the right proper holds a lotus. A Vidyādhara with garlands hovers in front of clouds to either side of the large lotus-nimbus of the goddess. Her head is surmounted by a lotus-pod canopy.

56.75.29

Cream sandstone. Upper part of image damaged; weathered 1′ 8⅜″ x 1′ 7$\frac{1}{16}$″

77. NIMBATE HEAD OF DIVINITY *Khajurāho, tenth to eleventh century.*

(PLATE 35)

(Cf. the tufts on either side of the smooth hair framing the forehead with 76 and 70.)

56.75.33

Published: *Philadelphia Museum Bulletin,* LII (1957), 37.
Buff sandstone. Slightly battered 7″ x 7″

78. PROFILE HEAD OF NIMBATE ATTENDANT DIVINITY *Khajurāho, eleventh century.*

(PLATE 33)

The crown (karaṇḍamukuṭa) is wreathed with pearls.

56.75.35

Published: Stella Kramrisch, *Indian Sculpture* (London, 1933), Pl. XXXIX, Fig. 93.
Cream sandstone. 5⅛″ x 4⅝″

79. HEAD OF ATTENDANT DIVINITY *Khajurāho, eleventh century.*

(PLATE 31)

Gods of the lesser hierarchy are crowned with the karaṇḍamukuṭa of superimposed ring shapes which look like inverted bowls (karaṇḍa).

56.75.34

Buff sandstone. Weathered; lips damaged 2$\frac{15}{16}$″ x 2⅝″

80. ŚĀRDŪLA *Khajurāho, eleventh century.*

(PLATE 34)

The rearing lion-tiger raising one paw over the figure of a man crouching in a posture of attack and defence symbolizes the power (śakti) of nature. (Cf. the "lion" on the back of thrones, p. 88; and *The Hindu Temple,* pp. 332–37.) The image is carved above a console.

Inscription on right side of slab: *Caturām* (the name of the craftsman).

56.75.27

Buff sandstone. 1′ 4$\frac{5}{16}$″ x 9$\frac{5}{16}$″

81. SCENE OF DANCE AND MUSIC *Khajurāho, tenth century.*

(PLATE 37)

(Cf. the movement of the female dancer and the bearded drummer with that of the Gaṇa [65].) The dancer balances the movement of her arms, the right on her thigh, the raised left bent at a similar angle. The boy to the right proper of the dancer plays the cymbals. The figures are sparingly bejewelled and wear loincloths. Broad pilasters with widely spaced cyma and arris mouldings flank the scene.

56.75.25

Buff sandstone. Slightly weathered 11⅞″ x 1′ 5⅜″

b) *Haihaya School (Southern Central India)*

82. MAHĀVĪRA *Jabalpur, Madhya Pradesh, tenth century.*

Mahāvīra is the twenty-fourth Saviour (Tīrthankara) of the Jain religion. His role is similar to that of the Buddha.

The naked figure of the Tīrthankara stands firmly and stiffly on both feet (kāyotsarga). On his chest is the auspicious Śrīvatsa symbol. The hands reach to the knees. Below, the image is flanked by two small attendant figures. A worshipper kneels in front of each. Two flying celestials (vyantara deva) are on either side of the nimbate head of Mahāvīra. Above it is a triple parasol (the parasol being a symbol of exalted rank) flanked by two elephants, here symbolic of the clouds of the air ocean.

On the cloth draped over the lion throne which forms the pedestal is a Face of Glory (kīrttimukha). This "lion symbol" identifies the Saviour as Mahāvīra.

The image was part of a temple of the Digambara sect whose saviours have "the regions for their garment." They are sky-clad—that is, naked.

35.39.2

Gift of W. Norman Brown
Dark buff sandstone. Top defaced 4′ 4″ x 1′ 1⅝″

83. TĪRTHANKARA PĀRŚVANĀTHA AND TĪRTHANKARA NEMINĀTHA *Jabalpur, tenth century.*

The images of the two saviours of the Jainas occupy two adjacent sides of a buttress. They stand each on a lion throne, Pārśvanātha under a canopy of serpent hoods. The cloth over Neminātha's throne shows his coznisance, the wheel. The images are flanked by attendant, crowned devas holding fly whisks. In front of them is a squatting devotee with folded hands; on top is a series of umbrellas (chattravallī) flanked by elephants.

35.39.1

Gift of W. Norman Brown
Dark buff sandstone 2′ 2½″ x 10⅜″

* * *

84. SARASVATĪ *Find-place unknown, central or Western India, ca. eighth century.*

The goddess, seated in the posture of ease, right foot pendant, her hands resting on her thighs, has fruit and rosary in her right hand in varada mudrā; the left holds a book. Four folds encircle the hips, end of garment falls over left foot to center of triratha pedestal. A Haṃsa (swan) in low relief to left proper of image. The socle has a square dowel on the underside.

31.60.15

Gift of N. M. Heeramaneck
Dark grey sandstone. Head broken 6″ x 5″

RĀJASTHĀN AND WESTERN INDIA

85. ŚĀLABHAÑJIKĀ *Harṣagiri, Sikar, Rājasthān, 973.*

(PLATE 38)

The tree-woman (p. 13) is supported on a lotus console with lotus buds. The same conventionalised flowers are part of her canopy formed by the top of the tree. The stem of the tree with its scale-shaped nodules curves upward between the left foot of the goddess and the small figure of the dancing genie. The body of the tree-woman is flexed in the triple bend (tribhaṅga) while the feet are turned to the left as if she were moving. A long shawl falling over the right shoulder in rippling verticals to either side of the figure forms an intermediate relief plane and accentuates the modelled volume of the figure. Its curves are enhanced as much by the contrast with the long pendants of the ornaments as by the festoons of the mekhalā which cincture her thighs. The right arm raised behind the head of the figure is bent towards the stem of the tree and toward the left hand raised to shoulder height. A coronet with a Face of Glory and strings of pearls adorn the smooth hair. The long dhotī has an incised pattern of wave lines, whereas the heavier fabric of the loincloth of the female gnome holding aloft a lute (vīṇā) is indicated by parallel, raised lines, indicating folds. (Cf. Inscription, *Epigraphia Indica,* II, 116 f.; *Indian Antiquary,* XLII, 57 f.)

56.75.12

Published: *Philadelphia Museum Bulletin* LII (1957), 34.
Yellow sandstone. Hands broken; heads of attendants broken; slightly battered 2′ 1⅝″ x 11″

86. TWO WARRIOR YOUTHS *Harṣagiri, Sikar, Rājasthān, 973.*

(PLATE 39)

Armed with bow, a quiver of arrows, with a long sword, shield, and a kind of halberd(?), the two figures wear short loincloths and rustic ornaments. The long hair is tied in a globular bun at the back of the head. The folded ends of the loincloth are rendered in shapes as thin as those of the weapons and the strap of the quiver. The figure in back view holds two short sticks(?) to his mouth.

Ringed columns with āmalaka devices and pot-shaped capitals and a rooflet frame the group.

56.75.24

Published: *Indian Sculpture,* Pl. XXXVI, Fig. 88.
Cream sandstone. Upper part of figure in back view partly defaced; frame damaged 1′ 2″ x 1′ 1¼″

87. VIṢṆU *Find-place unknown, Rājasthān(?), eleventh century.*

The standing image of Viṣṇu holds in the upper right hand the club, in the upper left the conch, the lower left hand is in boon-giving gesture.

To the left of Viṣṇu a small male figure holds an indistinct object in the right hand; the left rests on something. The female figure to the right of Viṣṇu holds an indistinct object. These two figures are apparently the Āyudha puruṣas, the "personified weapons" or attributes of Viṣṇu. In front of them and below the hands of Viṣṇu two worshippers squat with folded hands. They are placed on a carpet or padded cloth that has a wave border.

Behind the Āyudha puruṣas, two pilasters show on their capitals the figure of a Deva with the gesture of fearlessness (abhaya mudrā) of the right hand and an object (fruit) in the left hand. On the sides the animal symbols of the throne include: elephant, lion, and makara.

The rectangular throne pedestal with lotus petals rests on four legs, carved in the round. The nimbate figure of Viṣṇu is also carved in the round.

The image is a version in stone of a metal image.

31.60.25

Gift of N. M. Heeramaneck.
Grey slate. Hands of Viṣṇu damaged 8″ x 7¼″

88. MALE ATTENDANT *Kiradu, Rājasthān, eleventh century.*

(PLATE 40)

The figure in back view had its place at the foot of a large female figure—which, as a rule, is shown dancing (cf. *The Hindu Temple,* Pl. LXIV and *The Art of India,* Pl. 149). A shawl is tied around the chest (cf. [89, 91]). A bead necklace, the hem of the loincloth, and the hip-belt are shown.

56.75.21

Cream sandstone. Upper half of figure only; left arm broken; nose slightly chipped 6″ x 5⁵⁄₁₆″

89. MALE ATTENDANT *Kiradu, Rājasthān, eleventh century.*

(PLATE 43)

The squatting figure in back view is almost carved in the round. Its position was up high, most probably on a bracket (cf. 56.75.21) so that the foot drawn up underneath the buttocks could be seen together with the superb modelling of this part of the figure.

The moustached, bearded head has its long hair tied with a bandeau and arranged in a large bun at the back. A scarf is tied around the chest. A knot raised on the hip girdle is a forceful accent. The loincloth has an undulating border design and parallel undulating lines. They indicate the way in which the thin striped cloth is draped and clings to the body.

56.75.19

Published: *Philadelphia Museum Bulletin,* LII (1957), 36.
Cream sandstone. Nose, arms, legs missing; slightly battered 1′ 1⁵⁄₁₆″ x 9⅞″

90. FLUTE PLAYER *Kiradu, Rājasthān, eleventh century.*

(PLATE 42)

The figure is without the usual smooth finish of surface.

56.75.32

Cream sandstone. Upper part of figure; left hand chipped 7⅞″ x 5¾″

91. FIGURE OF A YOUTH *Kiradu, Rājasthān, twelfth century.*

(PLATE 41)

A scarf is tied and fastened in the middle of the vaulted chest over a long and broad neck chain. A necklace, and a bow in the combed-back hair, are shown on this fragment.

One of the five ruined temples in Kiradu is dated in 1148 (H. C. Ray, *Dynastic History of Northern India,* II, 926) and appears to have been built as the last of the five temples.

56.75.20

Cream sandstone. Fragment of upper half of figure; arms missing; nose slightly chipped 8⅝″ x 5″

92. TĪRTHANKARA ŚREYĀMŚANĀTHA *Mt. Abu, South Rājasthān, ca. fifteenth century.*

The image of the Saviour stands in kāyotsarga. His hands reach down to cylindrical, postlike objects with streamers(?), on their pointed top. A round niche on high, ringed pillars with lantern-shaped capitals enshrines the image. Kīrttimukha and scrolls above. Animal symbols of the throne on left proper. A rhinoceros, the cognisance of this Tīrthankara, is incised on the base. Inscribed: *Arham[?] laja[?] pranamati nitya[ṃ]*. "Honor(?) Laja(?) adores ever." (Inscription read by W. Norman Brown).

31.60.1

Gift of N. M. Heeramaneck
White marble. Slightly damaged 1′ 8⅜″ x 8$\frac{1}{16}$″

93. AMBIKĀ *Find-place unknown, Western India, 1460.*

The four-armed goddess, seated with one leg pendant, holds on her left knee a child with a fruit in its hand. The lion of the goddess is below her left leg. To the right of the goddess stands a small figure holding in the right raised hand a fruit(?). This figure may represent the second son of Ambikā. Her four hands hold nāgapāśa(?), a staff triply laced, three flowers, aṅkuśa (elephant goad); and the lower left holds the child. The goddess wears a karaṇḍamukuṭa. Above her head, in a rectangular opening of the trefoil arch of the throne, is the small figure of Tīrthankara Neminātha seated in meditation with dhyāna mudrā.

The trefoil top of the back of the image is engraved with bodhi tree leaves and has a kalaśa (water pot) for its pinnacle. The rectangular pedestal has perforated arches.

The image has an inscription on the back of the frame (read and translated by W. Norman Brown):

Saṃvat 1517 varṣe phāguṇa su di 10 śukra osavāla-jñātīya-śra-erabata[1]-bhāryrā-pūri-suta-sū[2]-ṭādevābhyāṃ[3] śrī-ambikā kāritā. gotraja pratiṣṭhitā śrī-śrī-śrī-kamala-indra-sūribhiḥ

Translation:

"In the year 1517 of the Saṃvat era [= 1460 A.D.] in the month of Phālguṇa, in the light fortnight, on the tenth day, which was Friday, the merchant Eravata[1] of the Osavāla clan, whose wife is Pūri- and his son the sū[2] Tādeva[3] had [this image of] the holy Ambikā made. It was consecrated as a family [deity] by the thrice holy Sūri [abbot or pontiff] Kamala-Indra."

27.18.2

Brass. The eyes, the jewel of the necklace, the Tilaka mark on the forehead, the crown, niche, eyes, and mouth of the lion are inlaid with silver 9$\frac{1}{16}$″ x 5½″

94. VIMĀNAPĀLA *Amber, Rājasthān, ca. seventeenth century.*

(PLATE 50)

The head of a Vimānapāla or temple guardian is one of four such heads which were placed below the āmalaka, at the end of the temple tower (śikhara; cf. figure of Deul Cāraṇī [36]), in the four directions.

A Tripundra mark on the forehead indicates that the temple was dedicated to Viṣṇu.

56.75.37

Dark-green micaceous schist, speckled black. Nose chipped 9″ x 7$\frac{1}{16}$″

[1] might be parabata
[2] abbreviation for Sūtradhāra? (surveyor)
[3] might be yadevābhyām

95. FOUR-FACED ŚIVA LIṄGA *Sāmbhar Lake, Rājasthān, ca. seventeenth to eighteenth century.*

(PLATE 49)

The four faces of Śiva although carved almost alike symbolise different aspects of the godhead in manifestation. The "fifth face," being "invisible even to the yogis," is not carved.

The squat cylinder of the liṅga is rounded on top. Its curve is extended to the Jaṭāmukuṭa of the four heads. Its stylised skeins of hair are encircled by a serpent. The earrings are flat disks. The face is composed of planes cut at angles.

56.75.38

Published: *Philadelphia Museum Bulletin,* LII (1957), 38.
Whitish dolomitic limestone. Weathered
9⅛" x 10$\frac{3}{16}$"

96. DVĀRAPĀLIKĀ *Find-place unknown, Rājasthān(?), ca. mid-seventeenth century.*

(PLATE 51)

The figure stands with a slight bend (ābhaṅga) and wears a short bodice, sari-like draped skirt, and sash. The skirt is finely tucked on the right proper below a tight waistband. A separate piece of cloth is gathered in the middle and is tucked over the girdle in long perpendicular folds while the end of the sari is pulled towards the back. It clings tightly to the hip and covers the gathered skirt below it. The outline of this last portion of the sari is seen in a sagging curve below the belt, and in an ascending undulation at the bottom. The hem of the skirt is raised, curving up in scallops. A flat sash is taken twice around the hips, and is then arranged in large loops. The jewelry consists of several thin bead neck chains with ornaments in the middle and a broad, flat, garlandlike ornament reaching down to the belly (cf. 91). The armlets are flat rings. Some straggling skeins of hair fall over the shoulders. A veil forms a billowing foil to the right of the figure.

Similar figures of female guardians (of the gate of a temple?) are in the museum at Amber near Jaipur, Rājasthān (see *Kunst aus Indien* [Zürich, 1960], p. 189).

24.4.1

Bequest of Mayer Sulzberger
Buff sandstone. Head, arms, and feet missing
2' 7¼" x 1' 2⅜"

97. DVĀRAPĀLIKĀ *Find-place unknown, Rājasthān (?), ca. mid-seventeenth century.*

Similar to 24.4.1. The arrangement of the skirt is somewhat different, and the sash is absent. The garlandlike ornament is here a flat, beaded band, similar to that of the armlets. These are tied with a bell-shaped pompon.

24.4.2

Bequest of Mayer Sulzberger
Buff sandstone. Head, arms, and feet broken
2' 7½" x 1' 2¾"

98. DVĀRAPĀLIKĀ *Find-place unknown, Rājasthān (?), ca. mid-seventeenth century.*

Cf. 24.4.1 and 2.

The skirt is without the vertical frontpiece. It is gathered in vertical folds showing a deep vertical groove in front. The sash is looped in freely flowing curves.

24.4.2 and 3 are more summarily modelled than 24.4.1. The navel of 2 and 3 is cresecent shaped.

24.4.3

Bequest of Mayer Sulzberger
Buff sandstone. Arms, head, feet missing; slightly battered 2′ 6⅝″ x 1′ 4″

MĀLWĀ (PARAMĀRA DYNASTY)

99. ŚĀLABHAÑJIKĀ *Harsiddhi Temple, Candrāvatī, ca. tenth century.*

(PLATE 44)

The bust was placed on top of one of the pillars of the hall of the temple. The top of the tree bends its branches full of round fruits, right and left of the head of the goddess. The inclination of her long, oval face is set off by two different earrings. Her hair, overlapping the forehead, then taken back by a chaplet with a central kīrttimukha ornament, is gathered in a deep bun, half-covered with flowers. The left hand grasps pendant branches.

56.75.10

Published: *Journal of the Indian Society of Oriental Art,* I (1933), Pl. XIII.
The Hindu Temple, Pl. LX.
Cf. also: *Journal of Indian Museums,* XI (1955), Pl. VI, Fig. 2.
Deep red sandstone. Right arm incomplete; slightly battered 1′ 5½″ x 1′ 8⅝″

100. WORSHIPPING GODDESS *Vicinity of Paṭṭan-Jhalawar, tenth to eleventh century.*

(PLATE 45)

The main hands of the six-armed goddess are joined in worship. The figure is turned to the left (cf. coiffure and pearl chain with 99).

56.75.11

Dark grey sandstone. Auxiliary arms and legs broken; nose chipped 2′ 3¼″ x 10 11/16″

101. SADĀŚIVA *Candrāvatī, eleventh century.*

The triune head of this transcendental aspect of Śiva coalesces the separate faces by looping the matted skeins of hair from one crown to the next and by placing a shroud on top of the triple crown. This cover is tied with one knot in front. Two faces in profile flank the central front face. The faces are further coalesced, but also divided, by sharing one pair of elongated ears on the sides of the central face. The triune head was part of an image whose slab is rounded on top, following the contour of the head.

56.75.38

Buff sandstone. Slightly battered; weathered 9⅞″ x 1′ ¼″

102. VIṢṆU *Paṭṭan-Jhalawar, eleventh century.*

(PLATE 46)

The image has a faceted kirītamukuṭa and a small nimbus whose triangular indentations indicate rays. The necklace is studded with cabuchon gems. The chest is marked with the Kaustubha jewel which came into existence at the "Churning of the World Ocean." The sacred thread passes over the left shoulder.

56.75.30

Dark grey sandstone. Slightly battered 10 13/16" x 7 1/8"

103. VIDYĀDHARA AND CONSORT *Ujjain, eleventh century.*

(PLATE 47)

In his cloud-borne flight the celestial carries his consort who sits on his right thigh. Her body is turned forward, her right hand is raised in adoration (vandana). Both carry offerings to the divinity of whose image this fragment occupied the upper right corner. The figures are surmounted by a lotus (re: ornaments, headgear, etc., cf. Pls. 8, 11, 30, 38).

56.75.23

Dark grey sandstone. Slightly damaged 1′ 3/8" x 9 13/16"

CHAMBĀ (WESTERN HIMĀLAYA)

104. THE FISH AVATĀR *Chambā, eleventh century.*

(PLATE 48)

In his first avatār Lord Viṣṇu assumed the shape of a fish in order to save the world. The Titan "Horseneck" had snatched away the Word—the Veda—which had proceeded from the mouth of Brahmā, the Creator. In order to recover from the ocean the Veda, the lost Tradition, Viṣṇu took the shape of the fish.

This avatār is shown here as a large fish (matsya). The body of the fish is supported by a lotus flower which stems from a double lotus resting in the middle of the bottom of the panel. From this lotus base rises a pillar. Its length is filled with undulations of the wave design. The capital of the pillar supports the seated figure of three-headed Brahmā. On other branches of this lotus-tree pillar and in one line with Brahmā four deities are seated, on separate lotuses, each placed on a capital. With their right hands these gods grant freedom from fear (abhaya mudrā). On a lotus of her own, directly issued from the central lotus, the Goddess Lakṣmī is seated, below the head of the Fish. Her hands are joined in worship. Above the tail of the Fish, on a pedestal of her own, stands a skirted female figure (Bhū-devī? or the donor?). An indistinct shape is upheld by her right arm. On the tail of the fish is a semicircular object (a lotus leaf?). On top, at the level of the gods, two miniature temples are carved on the sides of the frame.

The symbols of the Fish, the World-Tree, and Pillar, and the lotus as the place of birth out of the Waters are combined in the design of the perforated window.

56.75.39

Dark grey talc-schist. Partly defaced 1′ 2 5/8" x 1′ 1/8"

105. RĀMACANDRA *Chambā, eleventh century.*

The Rāma avatār is shown crowned, nimbate, with bow and arrow. A long garland passes over the arms, fluttering ends of a shawl overlap the framing pillars. A worshipping male figure (Lakṣmaṇa?) kneels in front of the pillar on the right of Rāma; a female figure (Sītā?) on the left with raised arms touches one end of the bow. Above the cross-beam, carved in high relief above the pillars, are two celestials, right and left of Rāma's head. In this part of the slab the ground of the perforated window is solid.

56.75.13

Dark grey talc-schist. Very slightly damaged 1′ 3½″ x 11½″

SOUTHERN INDIA

106. NĀGARĀJA *Find-place unknown, Southwest Deccan, eighth century (Early Chālukya Dynasty).*

The Serpent-King holds a sword in his right and a lotuslike shield in his left hand. From the hips upward his body of man is held erect, below the waist a twice-coiled, reticulated serpent tail tapers into a point. The figure is crowned with a high karaṇḍa-mukuṭa and wears earrings, necklace, and belts around hip and waist. The sacred thread passes diagonally from the broad left shoulder to the waist. A thin line is incised around the waist. Above the shoulders rises a fivefold serpent hood. The innermost hood surrounds the head like a nimbus. On either side of the crown a symbol is incised consisting of a vertical wave with its ends curled inwards (cf. the outline of the lower, horizontal part of the Śrīvatsa symbol). On either side of the tip of the crown is a horizontal design of three (indistinct) pronged devices.

The slab behind the body of the Nāga King is rectangular; the circular serpent hood is flat at the back.

56.75.44

Clayey sandstone. Weathered; sword and nose damaged 1′ 10⅜″ x 11$\frac{3}{16}$″

107. GAṆEŚA *Find-place unknown, South India, ca. sixteenth century.*

(PLATE 54)

The seated figure of the "Lord of Hosts" (p. 12) rests on a dais with architectural mouldings. A mouse, the vehicle of Gaṇeśa, was carved in the middle of the upper moulding. Gaṇeśa wears a Karaṇḍa-mukuṭa, a ring around the trunk, a shawl wreathed in festoons over his shoulders, and a belt around the belly and anklets. His upper right hand holds the axe(?), the broken tusk is in his lower right, a ball of sweetmeat (modaka) in his lower left, the noose in his upper left. The trunk is turned to the left where it takes the modaka from the left hand.

27.18.23

Gift of Mrs. J. Norman Henry
Gabbro 1′ 6⅝″ x 1′ ½″

108. INNER HALL (ARDHA-MAṆḌAPA) OF A TEMPLE *Madura, South India, mid-sixteenth century.*

(PLATES 55, 56a–b)

The nave of composite monolithic pillars consisting each of a carved architectural unit and a pillar figure (55) leads to the door of the innermost sanctuary. Across the front of the hall is a transverse row of simple pillars (first pillar on left). The aisles are flanked by rows of simple pillars. (W. Norman Brown, *A Pillared Hall from a Temple at Madura,* gives a full account and reproductions of the pillars [Figs. 2–29] and the carved panels of the frieze above them [Figs. 30–37].) The pillars were assembled from two, possibly three, ruined temples. Four pillars are installed outside the ardha-maṇḍapa.

Amongst the small details on the shaft of the pillars the portrait of the architect (56b) with his measuring rod is noteworthy.

It is carved on the square part above the

base of the second, composite pillar on right. Portraits in relief of the architects in the building which is their work are also known from Western India. Some are inscribed. The bracket is on the last composite pillar on the right.

Gift of Mrs. J. Howard Gibson, Mrs. J. Norman Henry, and Mrs. Henry C. Gibson in memory of Adeline Pepper Gibson
Part view of Frontispiece, *A Pillared Hall from a Temple at Madura* (Philadelphia, 1940).
Granite. Height of pillars, approx. 8′ 3″. Height of details: approx. 1′ 6″

109. SOMASKANDA *Find-place unknown, South India, ca. thirteenth century.* (PLATE 52)

"Śiva together with Umā [sa-umā] and Skanda" (Kārttikeya) is seated in lalitāsana, the right leg pendant, the left resting on the seat with the knee touching the seat. Umā with left leg pendant is seated in sukhāsana, a posture of ease, the right foot resting on the seat, the knee being raised. The figure of the child Skanda, standing on a separate lotus, his right hand holding a lotus bud, is now missing.

Śiva with axe, the gesture of granting fearlessness, and giving boons (abhaya, varada), and an antelope (now broken); Umā with the gestures of holding a flower (kaṭaka) in her right hand, and varada in her left, carry their bodies erect. In Śiva's crown of matted hair is the crescent moon, on the left. The central jewel in front of his crown and of Umā's karaṇḍa-mukuṭa rests on a double makara, facing outward. A snake and dhattūra flower are further symbols in Śiva's crown.

The three-eyed god wears a makara kuṇḍala in his right ear, and a circular earring in his left. By their different shapes these ornaments show the male-female aspects of Śiva. Umā's elongated ears are without ornaments. Braids of hair fall over the shoulders to the arms. Three flower rosettes in Śiva's hair give a corrugated outline to his shoulders, whereas only one such very high knob near the ears accentuates the locks of Umā. At the back, the corkscrew locks of each figure are massed in a semicircle. A tassel dangles over the right shoulder.

Śiva wears a girdle around his chest. The finely pleated loincloth is secured with a belt. The sacred thread, necklace, and sashes cling to the body in broad, flat bands; armlets, wristlets, and finger rings are in higher relief; the armlets are spiralled with one end fanning out in scrollwork. The sacred thread runs parallel with the circles of the necklaces and then is curved forcefully in the vertical. The waist is taken in—on the figure of Umā it is marked by two "folds." The hem of her garment lies loosely around her hips (Pl. 7). Her striped, palmette-patterned loincloth covers the left pendant leg. The end of the cloth is folded on the right alongside the left leg. The treatment of jewelry and sashes is similar to that of Śiva. Umā however wears also an elbow ring. Her crown is the karaṇḍa-mukuṭa. A small lotus halo is attached to the back of her head. The backs of the figures are straight and flat, almost concave, yet firmly modelled; they are traversed by the sacred thread.

The sturdiness and compactness of this image, the "breathing" quality of the modelling, assign the image to about the thirteenth century (cf. *Journal of the Indian Society of Oriental Art* [1938], Vol. VI, Pl. VI, Figs. 1 and 2).

27.24.1

Bronze. Figure of Skanda missing; three fingers of left upper hand broken; tenon, left of Umā, broken; nimbus of Śiva missing; pedestal cracked in front 1′ 4⅝″ x 1′ 7⅜″

110. BHŪ-DEVĪ *Find-place unknown, South India, ca. fourteenth to fifteenth century.*

(PLATE 53)

The goddess stands on a double lotus pedestal on a double platform. The weight of the body rests on the left leg, with knee stretched and hip thrown out to left. The right leg with knee slightly bent touches the ground with full sole. The body is held straight, the right arm, slightly raised from the elbow, holds a blue water lily (nīlotpala); the left arm forcibly stretched in the elbow is held away from the body with the hand pendant. This typical posture of the bronze image of the goddess is here applied as a ready convention. (Cf. F. H. Gravely and T. N. Ramachandran, *Catalogue of the South Indian Hindu Metal Images in the Madras Government Museum* [1932], p. 73.) The conical karaṇḍa-mukuṭa of Bhū-devī is decorated with pearl chains and lotus petals. A lotus is tucked behind each ear. Makara kuṇḍalas are attached to the ears and rest on the shoulders. The outline of the exceptionally broad shoulders and heavy upper arm is accompanied by a string of flowers. A tassel and looped pearl string further decorate the shoulder. The locks, arranged in corkscrew curls, are massed in a semicircle on the back. A long pearl string is twisted below the breasts and passes over either hip to the back where it is crossed in the middle. A thin waist belt, armlets, elbow ring, heavy bracelets, anklets, and foot rings complete the usual jewelry. The armlets have each two central motifs, one in front, the other at the back, with a lotus flower in the center from which rise three lotus buds, while two festoons are attached below. The palmette-patterned loincloth fastened with belts and sashes is pulled around the right leg; the end is passed once more over the thigh. The end of the sash clings to the inside of the left leg. The hem of the cloth is shown along the left leg in the back. The tucked loincloth fans out in a semicircle above the belt in the middle of the back away from the body. Two folds on the chest follow the outline of the breasts. The pupils are marked.

22.69.2

Published: *Pennsylvania Museum Bulletin,* XVIII (March 1923), 9.
Bronze 2′ x 9¾″

111. ŚIVA NAṬARĀJA *Find-place unknown, South India, eighteenth to nineteenth century.*

(PLATE 57)

Śiva is the god "who sets everything in motion and who, absorbed in Yoga and enjoying highest bliss, is always dancing" (*Kūrma Purāṇa,* 2.4.33). The movement of the dance is from left to right, where the left leg is raised crossing over the waist and the left arm crosses the chest and the drooping hand points towards the foot. The right leg, bent in the knee, is planted on the prostrate infant shape of the Apasmāra Puruṣa, an embodiment of forgetfulness or ignorance. The creature holds in his right hand a snake which has fallen from the arm of Śiva. In the hand of the Apasmāra Puruṣa, the serpent, symbol of creativity, represents the egotism of the creature. The foot of Śiva, planted on the creature, is a place of refuge for those who struggle in the toils of causality. The raised left foot gives release (anugraha).

The upper right hand with the drum is a symbol of creation, of the primal vibration in the ether, which becomes sound and the word. The main right hand gives freedom from fear—the fear of existence; the main left hand points towards the raised foot; the other left hand, holding the flame of fire, the fire of destruction, balances the movement of the right hand with the drum. The upper part of the body is held straight in the vertical axis around which the limbs of the image are laid out.

The dancing limbs of Śiva are an image of cosmic rhythm swinging from destruction to creation in an aeviternal round which has for its axis the presence of Śiva. The orbit of the dance is the universe; its centre is within the heart of man; its purpose is release.

The three-eyed face is framed by a diadem demarcating the braids of hair of Śiva, the Yogin. They lie closely on the head and fall over the shoulders and the back. A crest of cassia leaves and the skull of Brahmā, dhattūra flowers and the crescent moon are the ornaments of his head. The diminutive figure of Gaṅgā—the river Ganges which fell from heaven to earth and was intercepted by the hair of Śiva—with hands folded in adoration is placed on the locks over the right shoulder, whereas a serpent rears its head on the left shoulder. The Makara earring in the right and the circular earring in the left ear are symbols of the male-female bi-unity of Śiva. At the back, the hair is laid out in eight separate straggling skeins. Ornaments, girdle, scarf, and loincloth are indicated by hardly more than raised lines. Around the right calf is a ring with a bell.

The rectangular pedestal has a lotus petal cyma. There are three holes across it, in the middle. The competence of this sleek version of the image of Śiva Naṭarāja stems from a form conceived in the eleventh century (*The Art of India and Pakistan*, Pl. 50).

22.69.1

Gift of Charles H. Ludington
Published: *Pennsylvania Museum Bulletin*, XVIII (March 1923), 9.
Bronze. Partly faulty casting (main left forearm, etc.); break across right forearms 3′ 1½″ x 2′ 2⅝″

112. OIL LAMP *South India, ca. eighteenth century.*

The lower tray of the hanging lamp is circular; the upper basin for the oil has four spouts for the wick; above is a knob on which the chain is fastened. A peacock decorates this lower end of the chain.

27.18.3a

Gift of Mrs. J. Norman Henry
Brass. 9″ x 9⅝″ (length of chain)

113. OIL LAMP
Same as 27.18.3a

27.18.3b

Gift of Mrs. J. Norman Henry
Brass. 9″ x 9⅝″

114. OIL LAMP *South India, ca. seventeenth century.*

The large circular basin rests on three legs. The spout in front has a flower in high relief on either side. Below the spout and clinging to the mouldings of the base is a peacock forming a cavetto along the vertical edge of the base underneath the spout. The tenons and a plate are at the back of the lamp.

27.18.12

Gift of Mrs. J. Norman Henry
Brass. 5½″ x 9⅝″ x 13″

115. DVĀRAPĀLA *South India, mid-nineteenth century.*

The four-armed figure holds in his upper right hand a lotus; the lower right is thrown across the body and rests on the club. The upper left carries the conch shell; the lower left is held in the gesture of admonition (tarjanī hasta). The weight of the body rests on the left leg; the right leg is raised to the left and rests on the club. A lion in front view is shown between the legs. On top of the crown (kirīṭa mukuṭa) is a Face of Glory (kīrttimukha) and from it "foliage" vapour streams horizontally. The panel was part of a wooden temple car.

21.38.1

Wood 1′ 2″ x 8″

116. DVĀRĀPALA
Cf. 21.38.1.

21.38.2

117. DVĀRAPĀLA *South India, mid-nineteenth century.*

Two-armed figure standing with slight flexion; the right hand rests on the club on right; the left is raised in admonition (tarjanī hasta).

21.38.3

Wood 1′ 6⅛″ x 6½″

118. BRACKET IN THE SHAPE OF AN ELEPHANT *Find-place unknown, South India, late eighteenth century.*

On a rectangular base with diaper pattern the elephant stands carrying foliage in its pendant trunk. A large rectangle is cut away between the back of the head and the back where the bracket was attached to the ear.

21.38.4

Wood 15¹⁄₁₆″ x 4³⁄₁₆″

ISLAMIC TRADITION (PAKISTAN)

119. DOORWAY *Lahore, Pakistan, early eighteenth century.*

The jambs of the outer frame of the rectangular doorway are covered with carvings in low relief, in four main vertical bands showing 1) a continuous lozenge pattern with inscribed rosettes, 2) alternating panels of one single octagon and three contracted octagons respectively, each filled with a rosette, 3) a continuous scroll, 4) alternating miniature pilasters and scroll panels (scroll as in 3). The patterns of the three last units are continued on the lintel as is also the fringelike narrow moulding on the outside of the three fillets. This narrow moulding—facing upward—as also the panelled, and the scrollwork fillet, are repeated on top of the first three units. The middle of the doorway is marked by a square composed of panels as in 2. The outermost band of the door jambs, carved with continuous lozenges, extends vertically to the top of the lintel.

The recessed inner door frame has for its main motif the lozenge pattern which here is extended from the jambs to the lintel. This motif forms the outer frame of the main decoration of the inner door frame, which is composed of a fretted design, the single fields filled with scrolls and octagons. The innermost edge of the inner door frame has a sequence of broad, pointed arch motifs with their base towards the door. The arches are filled with scrolls.

The two-winged door is divided into five panels on each wing. They are each filled with a bold geometrical continuous pattern, starting from a central rosette or lotus; the mouldings around the panels are studded with iron knobs.

30.20.a

Wood. 7′ ⅛″ x 5′ 7″

120. TRABEATE ARCH *Lahore, Pakistan, early eighteenth century.*

The arch is constructed of four projected beams on each side and is topped by a long beam. The front surface of the four beams is carved with arabesques on a pitted ground. The back surface is carved with a geometrical allover pattern. Each beam terminates with a bell-shaped pendant carved in relief and three tassel-shaped pendants of which the central one ends with the pointed snout of a gargoyle facing into the opening of the arch.

Socket holes on either side of carved portions of beams.

30.20.b–c

Wood. The arch has been split in two through the thickness of the wood 2′ 11″ x 6′ 1¾″

GREATER INDIA

121. SHIN ARAHAN *Find-place unknown, Burma, U-T'-ong, ca. fourteenth century.*

(PLATE 59)

Sculpture in the round. Shin Arahan was the preceptor of the Buddhist King Kyanzittha of Burma (1084–1112) and the Primate of the Kingdom. (Cf. *Journal of the Indian Society of Oriental Art* [1934], Vol. 2, Pl. XIII, Fig. 4; *Archaeological Survey of India, Annual Report* [1913–14], Pl. XXXVII, Fig. 58.) The figure of the monk, with hands folded in front of the chest, kneels on a rectangular pedestal which is carved with a double lotus. The monk's robe (saṅghātī) covers the left shoulder. A shawl (uttarāsaṅga) is worn folded over that shoulder. The lacquer was applied at a later date.

58.9.1

Gift of Mrs. Webster Plass
Wood, lacquered black, traces of gilding. Nose chipped 1′ x 3¾″

THAILAND

122. HEAD OF BUDDHA IMAGE *Thailand, Chieng-saen, thirteenth century.*

(PLATE 60)

60.22.1

Anonymous gift.
Bronze, green patina. Top missing 9½″ x 8″

123. BUDDHA CALLING THE EARTH TO WITNESS *Thailand, Sukothai, thirteenth century.*

Thai inscription of name of Chinese donor, Kim Ling T'ang.

59.93.98

Gift of Mr. and Mrs. Lessing J. Rosenwald
Bronze. Very slightly damaged, red patina with some green 12½″ x 10½″

124. BUDDHA CALLING THE EARTH TO WITNESS *Thailand, fourteenth to fifteenth century.*

The pedestal is a single row of lotus petals.

59.58.5

Gift of Mr. and Mrs. Rodolphe Meyer de Schauensee
Schist (?). Face damaged 5⅞" x 5½"

125. HEAD OF BUDDHA IMAGE *Thailand, Sukothai, fourteenth century.*

59.58.4

Gift of Mr. and Mrs. Rodolphe Meyer de Schauensee
Bronze, green patina. 4⅞" x 3¼"

126. HEAD OF BUDDHA IMAGE *Thailand, Sukothai, fifteenth century.*

59.58.3

Gift of Mr. and Mrs. Rodolphe Meyer de Schauensee
Bronze. Uṣṇīṣa and ears damaged 4½" x 3½"

127. BUDDHA CALLING THE EARTH TO WITNESS *Thailand, U-T'ong, fifteenth to sixteenth century.*

Pointed relief plaque. The Buddha, enthroned on Siṃhāsana with high arched back, is surmounted by a delicately drawn Bodhi tree. A vase with lotus flowers right and left on throne.

59.58.1

Gift of Mr. and Mrs. Rodolphe Meyer de Schauensee
Gilded tin. Slightly damaged 7⅛" x 4¾"

128. *BUDDHA CALLING THE EARTH* TO WITNESS *Thailand, Lopburi, sixteenth century.*

The image is seated on a high throne which has an inscription on the back; a triangular, leaf-ornamentation in front.

59.58.6

Gift of Mr. and Mrs. Rodolphe Meyer de Schauensee
Thin silver sheets over stic'lac. Slightly damaged and repaired 4½" x 2"

129. HEAD OF BUDDHA *Ayuthiā, seventeenth to eighteenth century.*

26.23.1

Given anonymously
Bronze, olive-green patina. Points of diadem and tip of flame broken 3½" x 2½"

130. HEAD OF BUDDHA *Ayuthiā, seventeenth to eighteenth century.*

26.23.2

Given anonymously
Bronze, grey patina. 3⅜" x 2⅛"

131. BUDDHA CALLING THE EARTH TO WITNESS *Northern Thailand, eighteenth to nineteenth century.*

The uṣṇīṣa (cranial protuberance) is surmounted by a high flame encircled by a lotus flower which holds a jewel.

The saṅghātī covers the left shoulder over which also the folded cīvara is placed.

45.57.194

Gift of Mrs. Harald Paumgarten
Bronze. 11⅛" x 6⅝"

CAMBODIA

132. PRAJÑĀPĀRAMITĀ *Cambodia, Khmer, ninth to tenth century.*

Standing with arms pendant holding lotus bud in right hand and book in left hand.

59.88.1

Gift of James H. W. Thompson
Bronze. 5¼″ x 1⅞″

133. BUDDHA *Cambodia, Khmer, eleventh century.*

Head only; surrounded by serpent hoods of Nāga Mucalinda. The back is covered by a scale design showing a lotus rosette in the centre.

28.21.1

Gift of H. H. F. Jayne
Buff sandstone. Broken along edges of upper part 4′ 6″ x 1′ 7″

134. HEAD OF BUDDHA *Find-place unknown, Cambodia, Khmer, end of twelfth to early thirteenth century.*

Style of the Bayon.

23.2.1

Given in memory of Mrs. George Tucker Bispham by her son
Published: G. Groslier, *Arts et Archeologie Khmers,* II (1924–26), Pl. XX.
Pennsylvania Museum Bulletin, XVIII (April 1923), 3.
Buff sandstone. Tip of uṣṇīṣa, ears battered 9¾″ x 6½″

135. MALE DIVINITY (KUBERA?) *Cambodia, Khmer, twelfth to thirteenth century.*

(PLATE 61)

With the right hand in abhaya mudrā, the left in vitarka mudrā, the figure stands firmly on both feet (samapādasthānaka) on a three-lobed lotus pedestal. The figure wears a hip-length cape, skirt, pointed crown, ornaments.

38.37.1

Bronze (green and blue patina). Hole in centre back of base 8″ x 2¹¹⁄₁₆″

Plates

List of Plates

* The numbers in square brackets refer to those of the Catalogue.

PLATE 1. Worshipper. Bhuvaneshvar, Orissa, first century B.C. [1]*

* The numbers in square brackets refer to those of the Catalogue.

PLATE 2A. Head of an acolyte of the Buddha. Mathurā, Uttar Pradesh, second century A.D. [5]

PLATE 2B. Head of a royal personage. Mathurā, Uttar Pradesh, second century A.D. [6]

PLATE 3. Worshipping Yakṣī. Mathurā, Uttar Pradesh, second half, first century. [7]

PLATE 4. Scenes on a railing post. Mathurā, Uttar Pradesh, second century. [11]

PLATE 5A. Head of a Bodhisattva, Gandhāra, Pakistan, fourth century. [20]

PLATE 5B. Head of a Bodhisattva. Afghanistan, fifth century. [21]

PLATE 6. Nāga in lotus pond. Bhuvaneshvar, Orissa, early eighth century. [29]

PLATE 7. Sakhī. Bhuvaneshvar, Orissa, early eighth century. [30]

PLATE 8. Durgā killing the Buffalo Titan. Bhuvaneshvar, later part, eighth century. [31]

PLATE 9. Kārttikeya. Puri, Orissa, eleventh century. [32]

PLATE 10. Head of Kārttikeya. Detail of 9.

PLATE 11. Vidyādhara. Detail of 9.

PLATE 12. Khasarpaṇa Lokeśvara. Chauduar, Orissa, twelfth century. [33]

PLATE 13. Tārā and Sūcīmukha. Detail of pedestal of 12.

PLATE 14. Mithuna. Bhuvaneshvar, Orissa, late eleventh century. [34]

PLATE 15. Boar, foliage, and scrolls. Koṇārak, Orissa, mid-thirteenth century. [35]

PLATE 16. Deul Cāraṇī. Koṇārak, Orissa, mid-thirteenth century. [36]

PLATE 17. Mithuna. Orissa, thirteenth century. [37]

PLATE 18. Detail of 17.

PLATE 19. Buddha subdues the raging elephant Nālagiri. Bihār, second half, ninth century. [41]

PLATE 20. Crowned Buddha, preaching. Bodh-gayā, Bihār, eleventh century. [45]

PLATE 21. Nāga Mithuna. Bihār, tenth century. [60]

PLATE 22. Caṇḍī. North Bengal, eleventh century. [62]

PLATE 23. Detail of 22.

PLATE 24. Sūrya. Gaṅga Sāgarī, Bengal, late twelfth century. [63]

PLATE 25. Detail of 24.

PLATE 26. Dancing Gaṇa. Vārāṇasī, Uttar Pradesh, eleventh century. [65]

PLATE 27. Disciples conversing. Vicinity of Allahabad, Uttar Pradesh, eleventh century. [68]

PLATE 28. Head of Śiva image. Vicinity of Allahabad, Uttar Pradesh, eleventh century. [67]

PLATE 29. Umā-Maheśvara. Khajurāho, Madhya Pradesh, eleventh century. [72]

PLATE 30. Gaṇeśa and Śakti. Khajurāho, tenth century. [73]

PLATE 31. Head of attendant divinity. Khajurāho, eleventh century. [79]

PLATE 32. Kubera. Khajurāho, tenth to eleventh century. [75]

PLATE 33. Nimbate head of attendant divinity. Khajurāho, eleventh century. [78]

PLATE 34. Śārdūla. Khajurāho, eleventh century. [80]

PLATE 35. Nimbate head of divinity. Khajurāho, tenth to eleventh century. [77]

PLATE 36. Devī. Khajurāho, tenth century. [76]

PLATE 37. Scene of dance and music. Khajurāho, tenth century. [81]

PLATE 38. Śālabhañjikā. Harṣagiri, Rājasthān, 973 A.D. [85]

PLATE 39. Two warrior youths. Harṣagiri, Rājasthān, 973 A.D. [86]

PLATE 40. Male attendant. Kiradu, Rājasthān, eleventh century. [88]

PLATE 41. Figure of a youth. Kiradu, Rājasthān, twelfth century. [91]

PLATE 42. Flute player. Kiradu, Rājasthān, eleventh century. [90]

PLATE 43. Male attendant. Kiradu, Rājasthān, eleventh century. [89]

Plate 44. Śālabhañjikā. Candrāvatī, Mālwā, ca. tenth century. [99]

PLATE 45. Worshipping goddess. Vicinity of Jhalawar, Mālwā, tenth to eleventh century. [100]

PLATE 46. Viṣṇu. Vicinity of Jhalawar, Mālwā, eleventh century. [102]

PLATE 47. Vidyādhara and consort. Ujjain, Mālwā, eleventh century. [103]

PLATE 48. The Fish Avatār. Chambā, Western Himalaya, eleventh century. [104]

PLATE 49. Four-faced Śiva Liṅga. Sāmbhar Lake, Rājasthān, ca. seventeenth to eighteenth century. [95]

PLATE 50. Vimānapāla. Amber, Rājasthān, ca. seventeenth century. [94]

PLATE 51. Dvārapālikā. Find-place unknown (Rājasthān?), ca. mid-seventeenth century. [96]

PLATE 52. Somaskanda. South India, ca. thirteenth century. [109]

PLATE 53. Bhū-devī. South India, fourteenth to fifteenth century. [110]

PLATE 54. Gaṇeśa. South India, ca. sixteenth century. [107]

Plate 55. Pillars in Ardhamaṇḍapa. Madura, South India, mid-sixteenth century. [108]

a) Bracket with lion, bird, and vegetation forms.

PLATE 56. Carvings on pillars of 55.

b) Portrait figure of the architect of the ardhamaṇḍapa on lower part of pillar.

PLATE 57. Śiva Naṭarāja. South India, eighteenth to nineteenth century. [111]

PLATE 58. Gaja-Siṃha. Orissa, twelfth to thirteenth century. [39]

PLATE 59. Shin Arahan. Burma, ca. fourteenth century. [121]

PLATE 60. Head of Buddha image. Thailand, thirteenth century. [122]

Selected Bibliography

General

A. K. Coomaraswamy, *History of Indian and Indonesian Art,* London, 1950

K. Fischer, *Schöpfungen indischer Kunst,* Köln, 1959

H. Goetz, *India* (*Art of the World*), New York, 1959

Stella Kramrisch, *Indian Sculpture,* Calcutta, 1933

———, *The Art of India,* London, 1955

P. Rambach, and V. de Golish, *The Golden Age of Indian Art,* New York, 1955

B. Rowland, *The Art and Architecture of India,* Baltimore, 1953

H. Zimmer, *The Art of Indian Asia,* ed. J. Campbell, New York, 1955

Ancient Indian Art

Sir John H. Marshall, *Mohenjo-Daro and the Indus Civilisation,* London, 1931 (3 vols.)

Heinz Mode, *Das Frühe Indien,* Stuttgart, 1959

Stuart Piggott, *Prehistoric India,* New York, 1950

Sir Mortimer Wheeler, *The Indus Civilisation,* Cambridge, 1953

Early and Classical Indian Art

L. Bachhofer, *Early Indian Sculpture,* 1929

R. P. Chanda, *The Beginnings of Art in Eastern India,* Calcutta, 1927

A. K. Coomaraswamy, *La Sculpture de Bharhut,* Paris, 1956

J. E. van Lohuizen de Leeuw, *The Scythian Period,* Leiden, 1949

Sir John H. Marshall and A. Foucher, *The Monuments of Sanchi,* Delhi, 1938 (3 vols.)

———, *Taxila,* Cambridge, 1953 (3 vols.)

———, *The Buddhist Art of Gandhāra,* Cambridge, 1960

T. N. Ramachandran, *Nagarjunikonda,* Delhi, 1953

C. Sivaramamurti, *Amaravati Sculptures in the Madras Government Museum,* Madras, 1942

J. Ph. Vogel, *La Sculpture de Mathura,* Paris, 1930

Temple Sculpture

R. D. Banerji, *Eastern Indian School of Mediaeval Sculpture,* Delhi, 1933

———, *The Haihayas of Tripuri,* Calcutta, 1931

W. Norman Brown, *A Pillared Hall from a Temple at Madura,* Philadelphia, 1940

R. P. Chanda, *The Bhañja Dynasty of Māyurbhañj,* Māyurbhañj, 1929

Krishna Deva, *The Temples of Khajuraho in Central India,* Ancient India 15, 1959, pp. 43–65

O. C Gangoly, *South Indian Bronzes,* Calcutta, 1915

H. Goetz, *The Early Wooden Temples of Chamba,* Leiden, 1955

Stella Kramrisch, *The Hindu Temple,* Calcutta, 1946 (2 vols.)

Eliky Zannas, *Khajuraho,* 's Gravenhage, 1960

Iconography

J. N. Banerjea, *The Development of Hindu Iconography,* Calcutta, 1956

B. Bhattacharyya, *The Indian Buddhist Iconography,* Calcutta, 1958

A. K. Coomaraswamy, *Yakṣas,* Parts I and II, Smithsonian Institution, Washington, 1928, 1931

T. A. G. Rao, *Elements of Hindu Iconography,* Madras, 1914–15

U. P. Shah, *Studies in Jaina Art,* Banaras, 1955

O. Viennot, *Le Culte de l'arbre dans l'Inde Ancienne,* Paris, 1954

Journals and Serial Publications

Ancient India, New Delhi, 1946–

Archaeological Survey of India, Memoirs, Calcutta

Art and Letters, London, 1925–

Artibus Asiae, Ascona, 1925–

Arts Asiatiques, Paris, 1954–

Bulletin of the Madras Government Museum

Bulletin of the Museum and Picture Gallery, Baroda, 1944–

Bulletin of the Prince of Wales Museum, Bombay, 1952–

The Heritage of Indian Art Series, Bombay, 1957–

Journal of Indian Museums, Bombay, 1945–

Journal of the Indian Society of Oriental Art, Calcutta, 1933–

Lalitkalā, New Delhi, 1955–

Mārg, Bombay, 1947–

Oriental Art, Oxford, 1948–

Catalogues

a. Museums:

N. K. Bhattasali, *Iconography of Buddhist and Brahmanical Sculptures in the Dacca Museum,* Dacca, 1929

R. P. Chanda, *Mediaeval Indian Sculpture in the British Museum,* London, 1936

A. K. Coomaraswamy, *Sculptures in the Museum of Fine Arts,* Boston, 1923

F. H. Gravely and T. N. Ramachandran, *Catalogue of South Indian Hindu Metal Images in the Madras Museum,* 1932

N. G. Majumdar, *A Guide to the Sculptures in the Indian Museum* (Calcutta), New Delhi, 1937

D. R. Sahni and J. Ph. Vogel, *Catalogue of the Museum of Archaeology at Sarnath,* Calcutta, 1914

C. Sivaramamurti, *A Guide to the Archaeological Gallery of the Indian Museum,* Calcutta, 1954

b. Exhibitions:

The Art of India and Pakistan, London, 1949 (ed. L. Ashton, Sculpture: K. de B. Codrington and J. Irwin)

Gandhara Sculpture from Pakistan Museums, New York, 1960 (B. Rowland)

Kunst aus Indien, Zürich, 1959 (H. Goetz, K. Fischer)

Bibliographies

Annual Bibliography of Indian Archaeology, Leiden, 1926–

Council of World Archaeology (Area 16), Cambridge, Mass., 1958–

A. K. Coomaraswamy, *Bibliographies of Indian Art,* Boston, 1925

B. Rowland, *The Harvard Outline and Reading Lists for Oriental Art,* Cambridge, Mass., 1952

Index

Index